THE ESSENTIAL LAVENDER

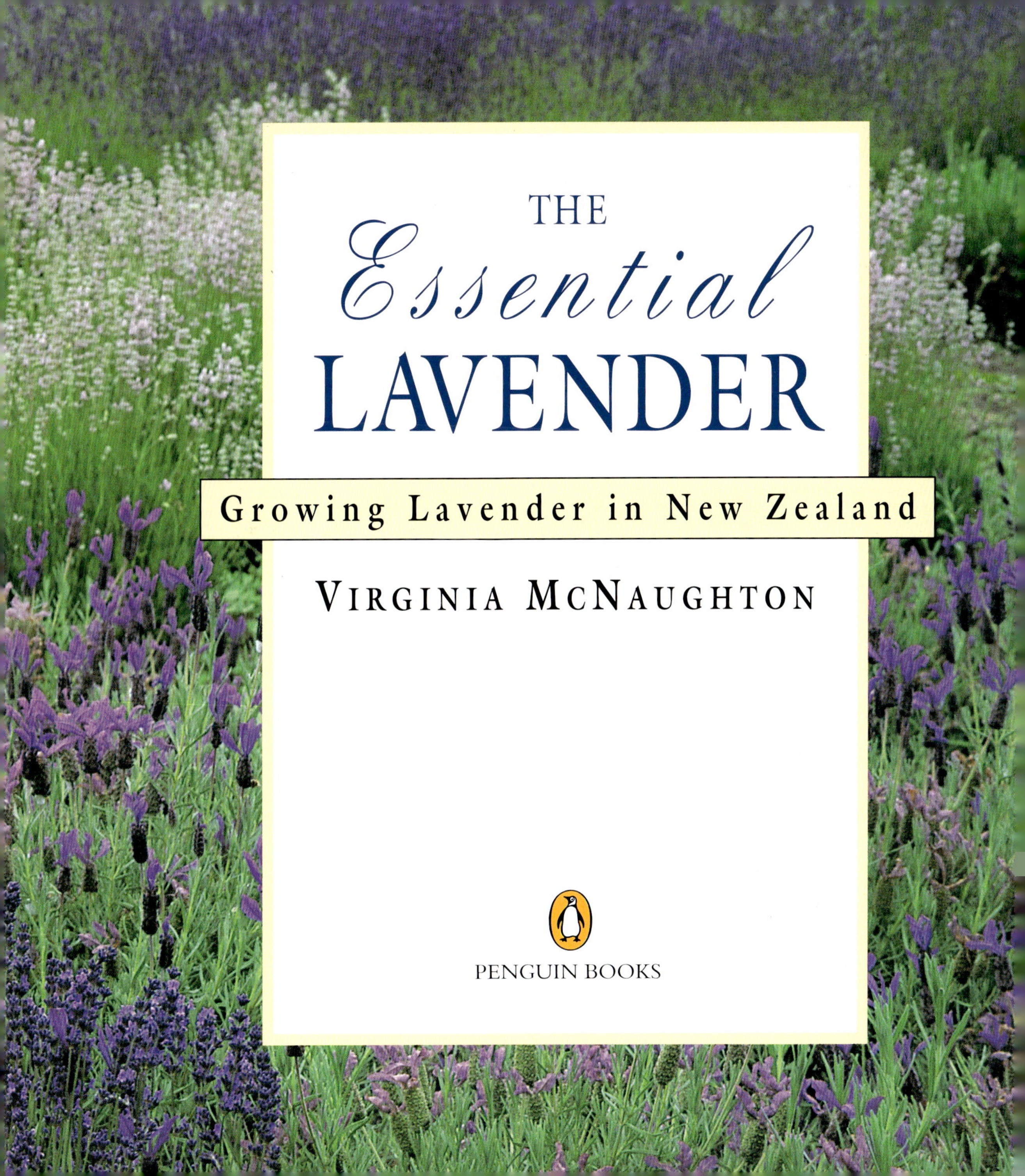

THE *Essential* LAVENDER

Growing Lavender in New Zealand

VIRGINIA McNAUGHTON

PENGUIN BOOKS

To Avice Hill, an avid herb and lavender grower who has given joy and inspiration to many people.

The author wishes to thank the following: Ruth Bookman, Jim Curnow, Molly Duncan, Betty Frost, Geoff and Adair Genge, Andrew Hodge, Dennis Hughes, Jenny McGimpsey, Judyth McLeod, Craig McWilliams, Gilian Painter, Peter Smale and Clive Wallis, the staff at the Manurewa Botanic Gardens, Auckland, and Rob Cross of the Royal Botanic Gardens, Melbourne.

The author would also like to acknowledge Arthur Tucker and Karel Hensen for their research into Spica cultivars.

Thanks also to editor Phillip Ridge, and the photographers Rosemary Dahl and Norman Zammit.

A special thanks to Rosemary Holmes of the Yuulong Lavender Estate, and Peter Carter and Bill Sykes for their valuable information and time.

Penguin Books (NZ) Ltd would also like to thank Ruth Bookman, Peter Carter, Gilian Painter, and the staff of the Manurewa Botanic Gardens, Auckland, for their assistance and advice during photography.

The author would like to advise that the plant known as *L. x intermedia* 'Grosso' is being sold on the Australasian market as *L. x intermedia* 'Dilly Dilly'. Also, that the plants *L. x intermedia* 'Super' and *L. x intermedia* 'Impress Purple' are being sold under the name *L. x intermedia* 'Arabian Night'. Similarly, on the Australasian market *L. x intermedia* 'Sussex' is *L. x intermedia* 'Super', the tall growing L. x intermedia 'Grey Lady' is *L. x intermedia* 'Seal', and *L. a* 'Avice Hill' is synonymous with *L. a* 'Impression'.

PENGUIN BOOKS

Penguin Books (NZ) Ltd, cnr Airborne and Rosedale Roads, Albany, Auckland 1310, New Zealand
Penguin Books Ltd, 27 Wrights Lane, London W8 5TZ, England
Penguin USA, 375 Hudson Street, New York, NY 10014, United States
Penguin Books Australia Ltd, 487 Maroondah Highway, Ringwood, Australia 3134
Penguin Books Canada Ltd, 10 Alcorn Avenue, Toronto, Ontario, Canada M4V 3B2
Penguin Books (South Africa) Pty Ltd, 4 Pallinghurst Road, Parktown, Johannesburg 2193, South Africa

Penguin Books Ltd, Registered Offices: Harmondsworth, Middlesex, England

First published by Penguin Books (NZ) Ltd, 1994, reprinted 1995
This edition published 1999

5 7 9 10 8 6 4 2

Text © Virginia McNaughton, 1994

Photographs © as credited where they appear. Front cover photograph © Rosemary Dahl; photographs on pp. 6, 76 and 77 by Norman Zammit © Penguin Books (NZ) Ltd; photographs on pp. 61 and 65 © Gil Hanly.

Designed by Philip Ridge
Typeset by Seven, Auckland
Printed in Hong Kong by Condor Production

All rights reserved. Without limiting the rights under copyright reserved above, no part of this publication may be reproduced, stored in or introduced into a retrieval system, or transmitted, in any form or by any means (electronic, mechanical, photocopying, recording or otherwise), without the prior written permission of both the copyright owner and the above publisher of this book.

Contents

Lavender Lore and Legend / 7

Profusion of Lavender / 13

Lavender — A Gardener's Delight / 48

Creative Ideas with Lavender / 68

Specialist Lavender Nurseries in Australasia / 79

Select Index / 80

Lavender Legend & Lore

*'Everyone knows Lavender;
this knowledge is of all time and of every country'*

Baron Frederic de Gingins-Lassaraz, *Histoire Naturelle Des Lavandes*

OF all the plants in the garden, lavender is one of the best loved and most appealing. It is a plant that cheers the spirits of those who take the time to gaze upon its crisp, sweet-smelling foliage and fragrantly uplifting flower spikes. Just standing near lavender will induce a feeling of deep calmness and joyous acceptance of life.

It has always been an attractive addition to any garden and once planted encourages a steady stream of bees which is an added bonus to a keen vegetable grower or natural plant hybridisation enthusiast. William Lawson, who wrote *The Country House-Wife's Garden* in 1653, informs us that lavender is not only good for the bees but was 'the most comfortable flower for smelling except roses'.

It is hardly surprising then that through the centuries lavender has come to symbolise 'love and affection, cleanliness, purity, chastity, protection, longevity, acknowledgement, perseverance and peace'. Curiously, one of lavender's more interesting attributes is that of 'distrust' — believed to have been given because the asp, a poisonous viper, made lavender its hiding place. Thus, a certain amount of caution was needed by those gathering its flowers.

The word 'lavender' is thought to have been derived from the Latin word *lavare* meaning 'to wash' since the Romans made a habit of perfuming their baths with lavender.

The Greeks also used lavender but apparently more for medicinal purposes. Dioscorides, a Greek physician and botanist who lived in Asia Minor during the first century AD, seems to have been the first to describe *Lavandula stoechas* as 'an herb with slender twiggs having ye haire like tyme, but yet longer leaved'. In his *Materia Medica*, written in AD 60, he attributed it with having 'deobstruent and roborant [laxative and stimulant] qualities' which enabled it to be used for chest complaints. He never actually mentioned lavender by name but always referred to it as *'stoechas'* which is now more commonly called French or Italian lavender. *'Stoechas'*, he said, 'grows near Gaul in the Islands called Stoechades from whence comes its name.' These Islands are now called Iles de Hyeres and *L. stoechas* still grows there today.

The Greeks were credited with giving to lavender the name *Nardus*, derived from a town in Syria called Naarda. The name was shortened to 'nard'. The Romans also imported a plant called nard *(Nardus italica)* from India to perfume their baths and use as a hair and body oil. Pliny the Elder mentioned a plant called false nard or pseudo-nardus which Baron Frederic de Gingins-Lassaraz in his book *Natural History of the Lavenders* took to be lavender. It seems that Pliny may have distinguished between *L. stoechas* (French lavender) and what we now call the English-type lavender (formerly known as *L. spica*). The Romans used *L. stoechas* medicinally and the oil of *L. spica* to extend their precious imported oils. Lavender may have eventually replaced the use of some of these precious oils.

From the sixth century the Byzantine Empire and later the Arabs maintained the Greek and Roman medicinal uses of lavender. The early Arabs continued using the flowers as an expectorant and antispasmodic. Lavender water applied to the skin maintains tone and freshness and Arab women used lavender vinegar on their cheeks instead of rouge to give colour.

The medieval herb or physic garden from Petrarca's Trostspiegel, *1531. Lavender has always been prized for its medicinal qualities.*

They also used a powder of lavender and sweet basil to perfume their hair. Avicenne, an Arab writer living in the eleventh century, mentions a plant whose description resembles that of *L. dentata* (toothed lavender) and says that it had 'virtues similar to those of *L. stoechas*'.

Lavender, along with other herbs, was probably introduced to France by Charlemagne around AD 800. He was responsible for drawing up the plans for a physic garden for the seventh-century Benedictine monastery at St. Gall, Switzerland.

Throughout Europe, herbal knowledge was maintained by the monks who laid out often extensive and specialised gardens in their monastery grounds. Herbs were grown for kitchen and infirmary usage but other areas may have included orchards, beverage-making herbs and gardens of scented and cleansing herbs.

During the twelfth and thirteenth centuries, gardens were divided into small areas similar to those of the monasteries but with less specialisation. Seats and arbours were prevalent and lavender may have been grown in pots or narrow fenced-off areas. Towards the end of the fifteenth century, the Italian influence crept into the gardens of the French and statues and formality became a feature. Parterres were developed in France and knot gardens in Holland. During the fifteenth century through to the seventeenth, England developed its own form of knot garden and lavender was often one of the hedging plants used to outline delicate and often complicated designs.

Details of when lavender arrived in England are somewhat sketchy. It was definitely mentioned in Turner's Herbal of 1568 and it may well have been in England 100 years earlier. However, it is quite possible that the ancient Celts introduced the plant to England thousands of years before Christ was born. Lavenders certainly grew well there and became very popular especially during Elizabethan times. Elizabeth I was said to have always had a bowl of lavender conserve on her table.

An early nineteenth-century lavender seller in London.

In later times Henrietta Maria, wife of Charles I, demonstrated a fondness for white lavender, having bowls of it placed in her apartments.

By the eighteenth century herbs were being replaced with ornamentals in English gardens and were often grown in vegetable plots separated from the new exotics being imported into England at that time. Most gardens were reduced in size and with the Industrial Revolution culinary herbs and vegetables were supplied to urban dwellers so they did not have to grow their own. In the cities street sellers plied their herbal wares and one of the famous street cries was:

'Sixteen good bunches a penny! Blooming lavender!
Blooming lavender!
Who'll buy sixteen good bunches a penny?
Blooming lavender! Lavender!'

At this time it appears that oil of spic or aspic, made from *L. latifolia* (formerly *L. spica*), was used in the preparation of quick-drying varnishes and by porcelain painters for diluting delicate colours. This oil was produced in large quantities in southern France and Spain. Baron Frederic de Gingins-Lassaraz described how shepherds living in Provence distilled the oil, poured it into leather bottles and from there transferred it to copper pitchers where it sold for '12 or 13 sous de France'.

With the advent of the World War I, herb growing became a serious business. Medicinal plants could no longer be imported into England so chemists urgently needed a supply from which to make their medicines. Maude Grieve trained many people in the art of growing, drying and preparing herbs for the industry. In 1931, she produced a standard work, *A Modern Herbal*, with detailed descriptions of the growing and usage of herbs, including an informative section on lavenders. Her efforts did much to revive interest in herbs in general to the point where herb growing has now become both a profitable business and interesting pastime. Collections of different herbs, including lavender, are now grown in many countries, providing valuable knowledge for the budding herb grower.

Throughout the centuries, a collection of lavender knowledge has been built up. Herbalists such as Turner, Gerard and Parkinson, like those before them, included in their herbals information on lavender, its growing conditions, usage and in particular its medicinal applications. The latter ranged from use as a cleanser and mild stimulant to treating toothache, childbirth, mild forms of epilepsy, worms, vomiting, jaundice, apoplexy, palsy, fainting, loss of speech and stubborn coughs. It was particularly used to treat symptoms of nervous disorder, headaches of nervous origin and 'brain maladies'. Charles VI of France (the 'Mad') had his white silk cushions stuffed with lavender — presumably this may have temporarily prevented him from thinking of himself as made of glass!

Similarly, Parkinson, a herbalist and apothecary to James I, quotes lavender as being of 'especiall good use for all griefes and paines of the head and brain'. Likewise a quotation from Turner, whose herbal was dedicated to Elizabeth I, states that 'the flowers of lavender quilted in a cap comfort the brain very well', and that it was highly recommended for all diseases of the brain that 'come of a cold cause'. In the *Hortus Sanitatis*, written in 1485, the author claimed that a mixture of flowers of *L. stoechas*, bay, betony, red roses, marjoram, clove pinks and nutmeg blossoms placed in a little bag on the head 'will soothe all pains'. He stipulated that for 'noblemen, it was to be made of 'red silk' and for 'common people' it had to be made of 'plainer stuff' — obviously all part of the healing process. *L. stoechas* was called 'sticadore' and was one of the ingredients which along with rosemary, wormwood, rue, sage and mint, composed the 'four thieves vinegar' used to combat the plague during the Middle Ages.

Over the years, lavender has been used extensively in healing and purifying rituals and for general cleansing purposes. The flowers burnt on the manor or house fire were used to induce rest and sleep and could be scattered around to promote a peaceful atmosphere. Lavender flowers were also used 'because of their virtue in protecting clothes from dirty, filthy beasts'. Hence lavender has been used to perfume linen and silk and to protect clothes and linen from insects, particularly moths. It is probably for similar reasons that an ancient tale relates that Mary washed the swaddling clothes of Jesus in lavender water, a tradition which continued through to Tudor times.

Benedictine Abbess Hildegard (1098-1180), who lived in a monastery in Mainz and was a strong visionary and well versed in natural science and medicine, mentioned that lavender was useful in ridding the head of lice and for clearing the eyes. In fact, lavender water was still being used as a delousing agent in 1874. Oil of aspic may well have been used in veterinary medicine as a means of delousing and removing fleas from animals' coats.

Abbess Hildegard also recommended lavender for deterring evil spirits. It was indeed burnt in bonfires for this purpose especially on St John's Day, 24 June, when many spirits were thought to be abroad. If one was particularly keen

Two apothecaries discuss the virtues of a herb (from a medieval illustrated herbal).

to see ghosts, then carrying a bunch of lavender was believed to aid the perception of such entities. When worn, lavender protected the wearer against the evil eye, especially true for children living in Tuscany. The Kabyle women of North Africa believed that lavender would protect them from maltreatment by their spouses.

The oil, rubbed on the person or on the clothes, was used to attract a lover and was particularly beneficial for any woman looking for a suitor, hence lavender's use in love potions, spells and for scenting writing paper. A famous beauty of the old French Court was still so beautiful at the age of 70 that her grandson fell in love with her. The recipe to keep her youthful was reputed to be as follows: 'Take a handful of dried lavender flowers, a handful of rosemary leaves, handful of dried mint, handful of comfrey roots, and one of thyme. Mix all together loosely in a muslin bag. Place in your bath, pour on enough boiling water to cover and let soak 10 minutes. Then fill up tub. Rest 15 minutes in the "magic water" — and think virtuous thoughts.'

Ironically, another use of lavender — and possibly worth trying only at one's own risk — was that pertaining to chastity. It was believed that a person whose head was sprinkled with lavender water would remain chaste as long as the lavender fragrance lingered. Apparently wearing lavender and rosemary together achieved the same purpose.

With such wide applications, it is not surprising that lavender has always been considered an essential part of the garden. Apart from its well-documented medicinal uses, lavender was also planted for its ornamental effect, particularly as a form of hedging — and here we are reminded of the intricate knot gardens, parterres and formal plantings of the European gardens in the sixteenth and seventeenth centuries. Yet, it was only with revival of the cottage garden tradition at the end of the nineteenth century that lavender assumed a more important role in the garden. Through the efforts of designers like Gertrude Jekyll and William Robinson herbs were once again mixed with older well-known plants, ornamentals and the newly introduced array of brightly-coloured annuals.

Lavender was certainly one of the first garden plants imported by immigrants to Australia and New Zealand during the nineteenth century, although it was probably valued then more for its medicinal and aromatic qualities. Even so, until recently no established garden was considered complete without at least one aged lavender bush framing the backstep or tucked away in the shrubbery of the back garden. And with the most recent cottage garden revival of the last decade lavender has been thrust into even greater prominence as an indispensable plant for every garden. This has coincided with the efforts of hybridists so that now gardeners are served a rich palette of species and their cultivars, of which over 30 are represented here.

There are now lavenders for every planting opportunity in the garden — as hedging, border plants, even topiaried specimens — in a flower colour range from greens, pinks and whites to misty blues and the deepest violet, with foliage colours from shades of green to the subtlest grey. These amenable, easily grown plants are indeed the gardener's delight.

℘rofusion of Lavender

'What greater delight is there than to behold the earth apparelled with plants, as with a robe of embroidered worke, set with Orient pearles, and garnished with great diversitie of rare and costly jewels?'

— JOHN GERARD, *The Herbal*

LAVENDERS belong to the Lamiaceae (Labiatae) family, a group of plants that include the mints (*Mentha*) and sages (*Salvia*). The genus *Lavandula* is divided into five different sections: Stoechas, Spica, Pterostoechas, Chaetostachys and Subnuda. Their distribution is widespread and extends from the Mediterranean region to include the Middle East, parts of west Asia and India, north tropical Africa, the Canary Islands and the Cape Verde Islands.

There are 28 species divided among the five sections, with the Pterostoechas section containing the greatest number. There are also many subspecies and hybrids and the number of cultivars is growing steadily. Nevertheless, most cultivated plants and those suitable for home gardens come from only three sections: Stoechas, Spica, and Pterostoechas.

General description of lavender

The distinction between lavenders is often very fine and depends on subtle differences of form. As such, the following descriptions are necessarily botanically exact — otherwise such distinctions will not be apparent. (Those unfamiliar with botanical terms will find the glossary and diagram on pages 16 and 17 helpful.)

All lavenders are perennial, shrubby, aromatic plants with either erect or spreading branches. The leaves, arranged in opposite pairs along the branches, are linear-oblong or spatulate to oblong-lanceolate in shape and the leaf edges can be simple and entire or dentate, pinnate or bipinnate. The leaves generally have revolute margins. The inflorescences are terminal, often at the end of short or long flowering stems (peduncles). These inflorescences are termed spikes and are composed of individual flowers arranged in a whorled fashion along the stem. Bracts are present and bracteoles may also be present. The flower is composed of an 8-, 13- or 15-veined, five-toothed calyx (often with appendage) and a two-lipped corolla which is generally lobed in appearance. Each flower has four stamens and a stigma composed of two flattened lobes.

THE ESSENTIAL LAVENDER

The height and width of lavenders varies considerably, depending on such factors as location, soil type, weather conditions and climate. This makes it difficult to indicate accurately a plant's height. Leaf size and peduncle length will also vary, often being shorter if the lavenders are grown under hard conditions or kept in pots for too long. The plant width can be calculated at between 1-1$\frac{1}{2}$ times the height of a plant.

BOTANICAL TERMS

The following terms are used in the text to describe precisely the various lavender characteristics.

bract	modified leaf at the base of a flower
bracteole	small bract borne on the flower stalk above the bract and below the calyx
calyx	outer petal; the calyces open to reveal the inner petals of a flower
cordate	heart shaped
corolla	the whorl of petals that comprise the flower
dentate	toothed or serrated
elliptic	oval
inflorescence	flowering structure or head consisting of more than a single flower
ovate	egg shaped
peduncle	main stalk bearing flowerheads or subordinate stalks
pinnate	compound, with leaflets on either side of central stalk
revolute	curled back
rhombic	diamond shaped
spike	flowers attached directly to and arranged along a stem with the terminal flowers opening last
tomentose	densely covered with woolly hairs

SECTION STOECHAS

This group is easily identified by the large, petal-like sterile bracts (rabbit's ears or coma bracts) at the top of the flower spike, distinguished from the fertile bracts present on the remainder of the inflorescence by their shape and size. There are no bracteoles present in this group. The fertile bracts are often rhombic-cordate in shape, 13-veined and hairy. Their leaves can be linear, elliptic, lanceolate or even oblanceolate in shape with entire margins, except for *L. dentata* which has dentate margins. Peduncles are unbranched and the whole plant may be covered in short hairs.

They are more frost tender than Spica-group lavenders and grow best in warmer areas. They are also more tolerant of humidity, but will not do well in areas with very high humidity or heavy rainfall.

In favourable conditions Stoechas-group lavenders will flower for most of the year with short intermittent breaks, one of these being around Christmas. The fragrance, however, is quite camphoraceous and not that associated with the so-called 'true lavender' or *L. angustifolia*. The section contains three species, a number of subspecies and various hybrids, some of which are described below. In the past there were four

16

PROFUSION OF LAVENDER

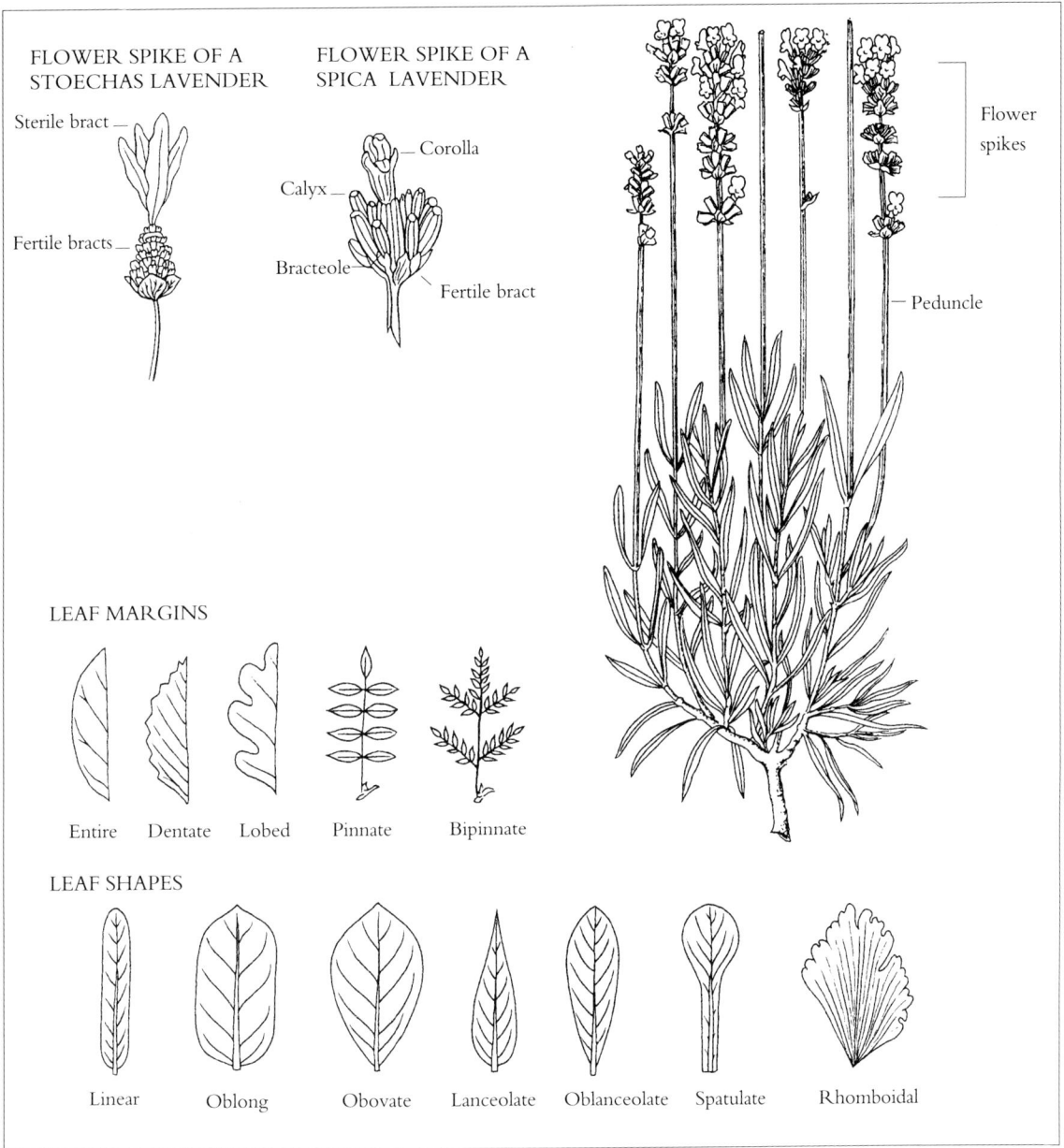

THE ESSENTIAL LAVENDER

PROFUSION OF LAVENDER

species but recently one of them, *L. pedunculata*, has been reclassified as a subspecies of *L. stoechas*.

NOTE: All Stoechas-group lavenders have been declared noxious plants in Tasmania and in rural Victoria.

Lavandula stoechas

This variable species is divided into several subspecies.

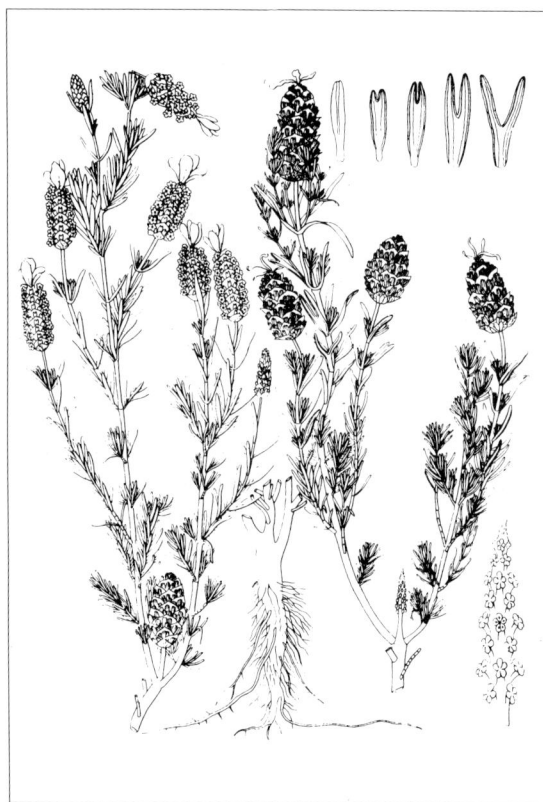

Lavandula stoechas ssp.*stoechas (from de Gingins-Lassaraz,* Histoire Naturelle des Lavandes, *1826).*

Lavandula stoechas ssp. stoechas

This is the best known form and is often sold under the common name Italian lavender. In historic references it was termed French lavender and some nurseries refer to it as Spanish lavender. All these common names are confusing and none really apply to the plant since of all the lavenders in this group it originally had perhaps the most widespread distribution throughout the Mediterranean region and North Africa.

In favourable conditions the plant can grow to 1 metre when in flower but is usually 70 cm when pruned. It favours slightly acidic soils.

The foliage is an attractive greyish green colour with linear-shaped leaves 2-4 cm in length arranged stiffly around the stem. In early summer it is covered with masses of small flower spikes on short (1-3 cm) peduncles. The compact, slightly square spike has prominently veined fertile bracts which cover the calyces. Initially the bracts are green but become purple veined as the flowerheads age. Dark violet corollas arrange themselves in a whorled fashion along the spike and 1-2 cm purple sterile bracts form the classic tufts at the top of the flowerhead. The whole plant is camphoraceous smelling and is covered in short hairs.

This popular plant, commonly available under the name *L. stoechas*, adds colour appeal to the garden and is always attractive whether in mass plantings or on its own. As a hedge it is easy to clip and flowers for a long period.

Perhaps one of the most hardy of the Stoechas group, it will withstand mild frosts depending on where the plants were acclimatised.

The flowerheads are not often dried but

make good pressed specimens or can be used to make a lavender vinegar for an antiseptic wash or hair rinse.

Lavandula stoechas ssp. stoechas 'Alba'

This white form of *L. stoechas* ssp. *stoechas* is very similar in growth habit, form and shape of flower spike — the main difference being that it has white corollas and white sterile bracts.

It is a vigorous grower thriving on added compost and quickly attaining a height of 60 cm.

Left: L. viridis; *right:* L. stoechas ssp. pedunculata *(from de Gingins-Lassaraz,* Histoire Naturelle des Lavandes, *1826).*

It will make a good potted specimen if repotted regularly but is planted to best advantage with other purple-flowered plants of the Stoechas group.

Lavandula stoechas ssp. pedunculata

This widely known subspecies is referred to as a separate species in older literature. Commonly called Spanish lavender, it is native to Portugal, North Africa, the south Balkans and Asia Minor although it is found mainly in Spain.

It forms a loosely sprawling bush about 60-70 cm in height and up to 90 cm in flower. The leaves are longer and slightly greener in appearance than those of *L. stoechas* ssp. *stoechas*. The greatest distinction between the two, however, is the length of peduncle and shape of the flower spike. Peduncles are long, 10-20 cm and occasionally up to 30 cm. The spikes are more rounded and plumper in shape than those of *L. stoechas* ssp. *stoechas* and the sterile bracts are longer, more linear-oblong in shape and violet-reddish-purple in colour.

This very attractive plant is not particularly hardy and needs to be sheltered in colder climates. It prefers chalky soils but will tolerate most free-draining garden soils, making it an attractive addition to any landscape plan.

Unfortunately, it is often mislabelled in nurseries or another plant is sold under its name. Frequently *L. stoechas* hybrids are sold under this name and superficially they may seem similar but *L. stoechas* ssp. *pedunculata* is quite distinct — it has longer peduncles and differently shaped spikes than *L. stoechas*. When the true form is seen in flower it cannot be mistaken.

A variable subspecies, it will often produce hybrids and forms resembling other subspecies when grown from seed, so is best to be propagated by cuttings.

Lavandula pedunculata var. *cariensis*, now known as *L. stoechas* ssp. *cariensis*, has peduncles of at least 23 cm in length, lobed calyx appendages and more pallid-coloured sterile bracts.

Lavandula stoechas ssp. *sampaiana*

An attractive subspecies that is native to west Spain and north and central Portugal. Its growth is upright and straggly and needs to be kept pruned. The fat purplish flower spikes are attractive, not unlike *L. stoechas* ssp. *pedunculata,* with long purple to pale violet sterile bracts. The foliage is greener, more delicate and finely linear than that of *L. stoechas* ssp. *stoechas,* with marked revolute margins.

During summer it seems to like frequent watering as long as it is freely drained, preferring granite soils as in its natural habitat.

Another subspecies, *L. stoechas* ssp. *luisieri,* is also available in Australasia, and is similar in form to *L. stoechas* ssp. *sampaiana*.

Lavandula viridis

Commonly called green lavender, this tall plant will grow to over 1 metre in suitable conditions. It is native to south west Spain, southern Portugal and Madeira. It is an unusual plant that will always create interest in the garden.

The foliage is green and sticky with perhaps the most camphoraceous smell of all the plants in this group. Both the foliage and stems are covered in dense, short green hairs.

Although called 'green', the corollas are actually white in colour, fading cream and brown as they dry, with green fertile bracts and greenish cream-coloured sterile bracts.

It will survive mild frosts and once established in the garden will seed itself freely.

Lavandula dentata and *L. dentata* var. *candicans*

This plant has been called the toothed lavender because of its dentate or toothed leaves, which make it easy to distinguish from other lavenders in this group. It is commonly known as French lavender in nurseries although it has a wide dis-

L. angustifolia ssp. *angustifolia*

tribution that includes Spain, Italy, Greece, Madeira, Canary Islands, Cape Verde Islands, Arabia, Algeria and Abyssinia.

Lavandula dentata has greener foliage than *L. dentata* var. *candicans* which is a more grey-leaved vigorous-growing plant. The latter is covered in hairs, hence the name *candicans*, and its flower spikes are slightly darker in colour than *L. dentata*.

The species tends to be variable in both the leaf and flower spike size even when grown in wild populations in its natural habitat. Variations can also exist with cultivated plants and in New Zealand, for example, there seems to be an intermediate form between *L. dentata* and *L. dentata* var. *candicans* that has grey-green leaves. It is also termed *L. dentata* var. *candicans*.

In warmer climates this plant forms a large shrub growing to 1 metre with ease and covered most of the year with beautiful lavender-purple (2.5-5 cm) spikes. The fertile bracts are green, heavily tinged with purple and the diamond-shaped or ovate sterile bracts and corollas are a delightful lavender-blue shade. The peduncles are usually long unless the plant is grown under hard conditions.

Avicenne, an eleventh-century Arab writer, gave the name 'Sucudus' to *L. dentata* and de Gingins-Lassaraz mentioned that the Moors of Valencia called the plant 'the fern' because of its lacy leaves. It is one of the most attractive of the lavenders in this group and during the sixteenth century in England was grown in hot-houses purely for its elegant form. The flower spikes can be used in floral arrangements, pot-pourris, wreaths and tussie-mussies. The plant itself makes

L. lanata

L. latifolia

a large compact hedge up to 1.5 metres in warm or coastal regions. It is also a suitable specimen for topiary.

It is not truly frost hardy so requires shelter in colder climates.

Stoechas cultivars

The following cultivars are probably crosses between the subspecies of *L. stoechas*. The foliage on most is grey-green and with their attractive flower spikes they are all worth a special place in the garden. All will survive mild frosts.

Lavandula 'Avonview'

A compact but vigorous-growing New Zealand-bred hybrid. It is 80 cm tall with impressive flower spikes on long peduncles. The sterile bracts are large and purple in colour.

The flowerheads are suitable for flower arranging.

Lavandula 'Helmsdale'

A lovely plant from Marshwood Gardens in Southland, New Zealand, 'Helmsdale' has compact foliage and will reach at least 80 cm when in flower. It grows perhaps a little more slowly than the other cultivars but the growth is luxurious and when fully mature it is a compact, well-balanced plant, requiring a minimum of pruning.

The flower spikes are a velvety burgundy-purple with shorter sterile bracts than the other hybrids. The peduncles are covered in soft hairs and are a good uniform length in an older plant.

The flowerheads are useful in pot-pourris and floral arrangements. It also makes a suitable hedging plant.

Lavandula 'Marshwood'

This plant, also bred at Marshwood Gardens, is tall and upright, over 1 metre in flower, and can look spectacular in a short time. The peduncles are long and very hairy just below the flower spikes.

The flower spikes and bracts are a delicate mauve-lilac with a touch of reddish-pink, and long sterile bracts. They fade with age so are not quite as suitable for flower arranging unless picked just as they come into flower.

Lavandula 'Pippa'

This New Zealand-bred plant will grow to 80 cm in loamy soil but less in sandy, lighter soils. Like many of the lavenders in the Stoechas group it is covered in spring with masses of flower spikes on short to medium-length peduncles.

The flowerheads themselves are at their best just as they come into flower when they will appear a striking luminescent purple on a still summer's evening. The flowers tend to lose their colour quite quickly as they age.

Keep well pruned as the bush has a tendency to sprawl.

SECTION SPICA

This group contains the so-called English lavenders — an unusual term since the species of these lavenders did not originate in England.

However, since they were introduced to that country they have certainly become part of the gardening landscape and many cultivars have been bred there and released on to the market.

Within this group there has been much misunderstanding over the use of the name *Lavandula spica*. In 1753 Linnaeus combined the then known lavenders into one genus. Many lavenders from the Stoechas group were known but the difference between those now known as *L. angustifolia* and *L. latifolia* was indistinct and both plants were included under the name *L. spica*. There ensued much controversy over which plant should keep the name. The more sweet-smelling lavender was given the name *L. vera* to distinguish between the two but it unfortunately continued to be called *L. spica*.

In 1930 at the International Botanical Congress of the Pharmaceutical Society it was decided to discard the name *L. spica*; the name *L. latifolia* was introduced for spike lavender and *L. officinalis* replaced the name *L. vera*. In more recent times the name *L. angustifolia* has replaced *L. vera* (and the defunct *L. spica*) but despite this, misnaming of these popular lavenders continues.

Lavenders in this group do not have sterile bracts at the top of the spike. Leaves are entire, generally lanceolate, oblong or linear in shape and usually covered in hair. Young leaves are often green or grey changing to grey with age. The spikes are generally 2-10 cm or longer.

This group prefers limestone areas and light, well-drained soils and warm rocky slopes.

The flowering times given here will vary from region to region depending on the climate.

Lavandula angustifolia
(syn. *L. vera*, *L. spica*, *L. officinalis*)
This species is divided into two subspecies: *L. angustifolia* ssp. *angustifolia* and *L. angustifolia* ssp. *pyrenaica*.

Lavandula angustifolia ssp. *angustifolia*
This plant, which is native to the western Mediterranean region, grows typically to 60-80 cm when flowering and produces fragrant violet flower spikes of 3-7 cm. The corollas are 10-12 mm

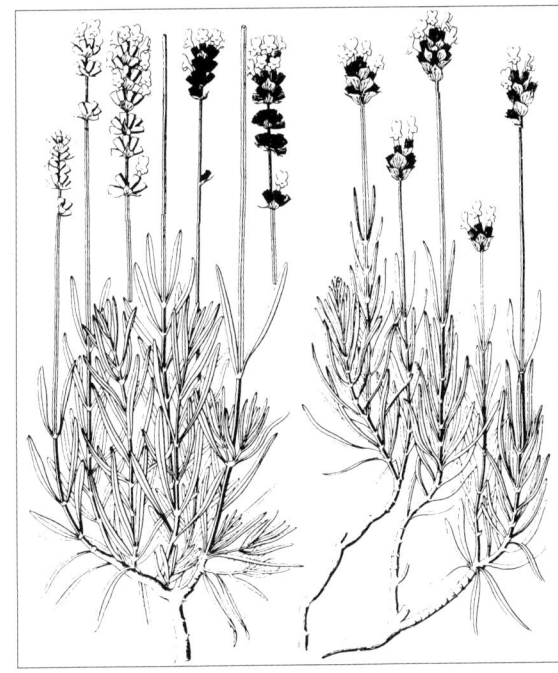

Left: L. angustifolia ssp. angustifolia; *right*: L. angustifolia ssp. pyrenaica *(from de Gingins-Lassaraz, Histoire Naturelle des Lavandes, 1826).*

THE ESSENTIAL LAVENDER

L. angustifolia 'Hidcote'

long with large lobes and the 13-veined calyces are 4-7 mm long. Fertile bracts are ovate to broadly obovate with pointed tips. Small linear bracteoles (0.5-2 mm) may be present. The leaves are 2-6 cm long, entire and linear with slightly revolute margins. The foliage is compact.

It is one of the earliest lavenders to flower, commencing in late November and continuing to send up fresh blooms for months. It makes a trim small to medium-sized hedge. The flower spikes are suitable for lavender bags and toiletries, floral decorations, pot-pourris and culinary uses.

This plant produces some of the best-quality oil, but because of its smaller stature and reduced flower production, hybrid lavender cultivars are more often used in commercial production.

Lavandula angustifolia ssp. *angustifolia* along with *L. latifolia* is thought to be one of the parents of the lavandin cultivars (*see* page 37). It also has a number of its own cultivars.

This subspecies is the only type of *L. angustifolia* commonly available in nurseries, frequently being sold under the incorrect names *L. vera*, *L. spica* and *L. officinalis*. Often these plants are seed grown and can be variable in form, further adding to the confusion.

Lavandula angustifolia ssp. *pyrenaica*

This subspecies, native to the Pyrenees and northern Spain, is rare in Australasia and is distinguished from *L. angustifolia* ssp. *angustifolia* by its large bracts — at least as long as the calyces and very wide. The calyces are 6-7 mm long with the hairs confined to the veins.

Lavandula latifolia
(syn. *L. spica*)

This plant, often referred to as spike lavender, is native to the western Mediterranean region and Portugal and is rare in nurseries.

Lavandula latifolia can flower up to 3 months later than *L. angustifolia*, in February. The leaves are 3-6 cm long and 1-2 cm wide and their shape is oblong to lanceolate, broad, almost spatulate. They are more greyish green and more densely covered in hair than *L. angustifolia* with only slightly revolute margins. The peduncles are 45 cm or more in length and frequently branched into three. The flower spikes are slender, occasionally interrupted. The 8-10 mm corolla tubes are purple and the 3-5 mm calyces green edged with violet. The bracts are long and 'awl' shaped with one prominent midrib. The 2-5 mm linear-shaped bracteoles are also a conspicuous feature.

The bush itself is not large, about 50 cm in height, but the flowering stems can add height and width during late summer. Unfortunately, the flowerheads do not have the sweet smell of *L. angustifolia* and the foliage has a distinct camphoraceous smell, much stronger than the lavandins. The scent is not unpleasant but it is powerful enough to clear a 'woolly head'. 'Oil of aspic' was produced from *L. latifolia*.

The plant does not have a long lifespan in the Australasian climate and at times can be difficult to grow. Occasionally plants turn black and die, so it is best to keep young stock in reserve. It is not as frost hardy as many of the other Spica lavenders and dislikes cold, poorly drained soil.

Cutting material can sometimes be difficult to obtain as the plant tends to become quite woody at the base and along the stems. It must be pruned carefully from an early age to obtain the best results, but is a plant worth persisting with and a valuable addition to any lavender collection.

Seed will grow true if obtained from a wild source or from plants separated from other lavenders. Sometimes nursery-sold plants are misnamed, probably because they were originally grown from seed of hybridised origin.

Lavandula latifolia and *L. angustifolia* are the parents of the lavandins and it is thought that the

Lavandula latifolia (from de Gingins-Lassaraz, Histoire Naturelle des Lavandes, 1826).

cross between *L. latifolia* and *L. dentata* produced *L.* x *allardii*. *Lavandula latifolia* is also one of the parents of *L.* x *heterophylla*. There appear to be no cultivars of *L. latifolia* itself.

Lavandula lanata
A beautiful grey tomentose-leaved plant, completely different from other lavenders in this group. Its common name is woolly lavender and it is native to the mountains of southern Spain.

Its leaves are 3-5 cm long and 1.2 cm wide — like a soft flannel to touch — and linear-oblanceolate to narrowly spatulate in shape. The spikes are narrow, up to 10 cm or more in length, and borne on long peduncles. The 8-10 mm corollas are dark purple in colour and the 8-veined calyces very pale by comparison. Bracts are linear or lanceolate and 2-5 mm bracteoles are present. The individual flowers open gradually, giving vivid splashes of purple along the spike.

The plant easily reaches 1 metre in height and width when in flower and is truly an impressive shrub. It has a deep rooted system and dislikes being moved once established. It prefers dry, chalky soils and sheltered positions, particularly when young. Rock gardens or raised beds make ideal habitats, providing enough space is left for its eventual volume.

When young it tends to be slow growing and can be difficult to establish especially if overwatered or planted in a high-rainfall area. It will survive frosts and even the odd snowfall. *Lavandula lanata* has a pleasant, slightly camphoraceous fragrance and generally flowers in late December. Its foliage makes an interesting contrast as part of a grey and silver garden or simply as a focal point.

The flower spikes dry too grey to use for floral arrangements and are not sweetly scented enough for pot-pourris.

Cuttings can be taken but need to be kept on the dry side. If the plant is growing independently of other lavenders, seed will grow true.

Hybrids exist with *L. lanata* as one of the parents and there are at least a couple of cultivars.

Spica cultivars
The cultivars of the spica group are divided into those with characteristics similar to *L. angustifolia* and those which are definite hybrids between *L. latifolia* and *L. angustifolia*.

Lavandula angustifolia cultivars
Lavandula angustifolia cultivars are often termed 'true lavender' and both the foliage and spikes generally display the characteristic sweet lavender smell. Peduncles are usually single and unbranched; if branches do occur, these are very fine and rarely form terminal spikes — there are just a few individual flowers in a loose rounded arrangement. The peduncles themselves are small to medium in length. Small bracteoles (0.5-2.5 mm) may be present or may have fallen off by the time the spike is in full bloom. The bracts are broadly shaped.

They flower about the same time as *L. angustifolia* or 2 to 3 weeks afterwards and although fairly robust in habit do not grow as high as some of the lavandins when flowering. Their spike colours range from lavender and violet through to white and pink.

Lavender and violet-flowering cultivars

Many of these can be grown for their floral and scented attributes and culinary uses.

Lavandula angustifolia 'Munstead'

(syn. 'Munstead Dwarf', 'Munstead Variety', 'Munstead Blue', 'Dwarf Munstead')

'Munstead' was bred by Gertrude Jekyll in England and introduced in 1916. It is similar in foliage and height to *L. angustifolia* ssp. *angustifolia* and flowers about the same time. The true 'Munstead' has bracts suffused with purple, giving the spikes a dark appearance prior to flowering. The corollas are a dark violet and the calyces are also veined in violet. When mature, the bushes will reach 45-60 cm in height. Flower spikes are continuously produced throughout the summer period.

'Munstead' is a versatile plant with uses similar to *L. angustifolia* ssp. *angustifolia*. It was traditionally used as Elizabethan knot-garden edging.

There is much confusion over this plant as it is frequently grown from seed with a resulting variation in plant form. The only way to preserve this cultivar is through cuttings.

Lavandula angustifolia 'Folgate'

(syn. 'Folgate Blue', 'Folgate Variety')

This cultivar, introduced in England about 50 years ago, grows to 60-70 cm when flowering. Although the appearance of the flowers may be blue from a distance, the corollas are more heliotrope in colour. However, occasionally a cutting from a stock plant throws a spike with corollas that are more blue coloured.

The interrupted spikes are 5 cm long, and the green bracts are tinged with purple. The plant itself displays upright vigorous growth and flowers within a week of *L. angustifolia*. In a good season it will have a second flowering period.

It can be used for floral arranging and as a hedging plant.

Lavandula angustifolia 'Avice Hill'

(syn. 'Hooper No. 10')

Raised in New Zealand, this is similar in appearance to 'Munstead' but will grow into a larger bush and flowers up to 3 weeks later. Flower spikes are produced freely and both these and the foliage are very fragrant.

The corollas are amethyst-violet with aconite-violet calyces and broad green bracts. The bracteoles are insignificant, less than 1 mm.

Plants produce a lovely hedge which continues to bloom after most of the other *L. angustifolia* cultivars have finished.

Lavandula angustifolia 'Bosisto'

(syn. 'Bosisto's Variety', 'Bosistos')

An Australian bred plant named after Joseph Bosisto, a nineteenth-century pharmacist who was one of the earliest manufacturers of essential oils in Australia. It is medium sized, growing to 30-55 cm when in flower with lavender-blue corollas on medium-length spikes. It flowers shortly after *L. angustifolia*.

Lavandula angustifolia 'Bowles Early'

(syn. 'Bowles Variety', 'Miss Donnington', 'Miss Dunnington')

This cultivar is sometimes sold in Australia and New Zealand under the name 'Miss Donnington'. It is of Scottish origin and was reputedly given to

Mr Edward Augustus Bowles by a Miss Dunnington — hence the confusion surrounding its name.

The true form grows 40 cm and up to 60 cm when flowering with lavender-blue spikes. The stems are straight and unbranched and foliage compact and grey-green.

Lavandula angustifolia '**Irene Doyle**'

'Irene Doyle' was introduced in 1983 in the United States. It has compact foliage and grows to 40 cm tall when flowering. It can be kept smaller with adequate pruning and forms a small compact hedge.

The spikes are more rounded in shape and about 2-4 cm long. Corollas are campanula to aster-violet and the calyces green tinged with a few purple streaks, producing quite a contrast in the flower spike. Bracteoles are almost insignificant, only 0.5-1 mm long if present. The fragrance of the whole plant is sweet.

It is often termed the 'two seasons lavender' since it has two definite flowering periods.

Lavandula angustifolia '**Lady**'
(syn. 'Lavender Lady')

'Lady' was bred in the United States, and is a most exciting find for those interested in bedding plants as it is one of the few lavenders that will flower in the same season when grown from seed.

It grows 20-25 cm high, 40-45 cm when flowering, and has compact grey-green, linear to oblong-shaped leaves and fragrant spikes of lavender-violet flowers.

The plants are uniform in size and shape and would make suitable annual or perennial garden plants.

Lavandula angustifolia '**Twickel Purple**'
(syn. 'Twinkle Purple', 'Twickel', 'Twickes Purple', 'Twickle Purple')

A larger-growing lavender bred in the Netherlands early this century. It easily reaches 60 cm and up to 90 cm when flowering but because it tends to sprawl, especially when flowering, needs to be well pruned in autumn. The flowers cascade around the plant like a fountain. On a mature bush the flowers are long (11-17 cm) and interrupted with dark campanula-blue corollas, aconite-violet calyces and striking green bracts. Flowering commences several weeks after *Lavandula angustifolia*.

Dark-flowering cultivars

This is an interesting group of cultivars for the home garden, used more for the colour of the spikes than for their fragrance.

They have greyer foliage and flower slightly later than many of the more blue-flowered cultivars. The calyces are generally dark aconite-violet and the corollas open a lighter shade than the calyces.

Lavandula angustifolia '**Hidcote**'
(syn. 'Hidcote Blue', 'Hidcote Purple', 'Hidcote Variety')

'Hidcote', released in England before 1950, is a spectacular dark-flowered cultivar growing to about 70 cm when flowering and covered in masses of dark violet spikes. The flower spikes generally dry compact and quite bulky in shape.

'Hidcote' flowers about 2 weeks after *L. angustifolia* and will continue to produce a few flowers after the initial burst, but it does not have a definite second flowering period. Pruning is required to keep its form.

It is much used in floral arrangements, pot-pourris, lavender dollies, pressed flowers, and for planting *en masse* and general garden display.

Although this plant is commonly available through nurseries, many of the plants sold do not have the true deep colour of 'Hidcote' and may possibly be from seed-grown sources. Another plant released on to the market called 'Hidcote Blue', which is also a synonym for 'Hidcote', tends more towards a blue shade and is not the dark violet of the true 'Hidcote'.

Lavandula angustifolia 'Nana Atropurpurea'

Introduced prior to 1923, this compact plant grows only 40-60 cm high and produces dark-flowered spikes on uniform peduncles. The corollas are dark campanula-violet, the calyces aconite-violet with bracts suffused with purple prior to flowering, producing wonderful dark heads — a slightly different shade to other dark-flowered cultivars. The flower spikes are 3-6 cm

L. angustifolia 'Irene Doyle'

L. angustifolia 'Avice Hill'

L. angustifolia 'Hidcote Pink'

L. angustifolia 'Folgate'

long and are interrupted and narrower in shape than those of 'Hidcote'. It flowers 2-3 weeks after *L. angustifolia* and has a definite second flowering period.

It is a very beautiful plant that makes a suitable hedging plant and lends itself to many garden situations. The spikes may be used for decorative display.

It is not yet commonly available in New Zealand and Australia.

Lavandula angustifolia 'Blue Mountain'

A delightful New Zealand-bred plant with greyer foliage than the other dark-flowered cultivars. It keeps its shape well and is very compact, making it ideal for lower-growing hedging.

In suitable conditions the plant will reach 60 cm in height when flowering and is a worthy addition to any garden.

Its flower spikes are compact and uniform in shape with reasonably long peduncles. The corollas are a darker shade than the other three cultivars in this group yet the spikes appear a lighter violet prior to the corollas opening. It will continue to produce spikes after the first flowering.

Lavandula angustifolia 'Gray Lady'

'Gray Lady', introduced in the United States

prior to 1967, grows 40-60 cm in height, producing dark-flowered spikes on long peduncles.

It has similar uses to the other dark-flowered cultivars and is one of the first of these to flower.

It can be difficult to propagate sometimes and must be carefully nurtured once the cuttings have rooted.

This is the true 'Gray Lady'. Another cultivar, 'Grey Lady', has been released on to the New Zealand market but is actually a lavandin.

White-flowering cultivars
Lavandula angustifolia 'Nana Alba'
(syn. 'Baby White', 'Dwarf White')
A low-growing, compact cultivar displaying grey-green foliage and producing fragrant 2-2.5 cm spikes on 6 cm peduncles. The corollas are white, the calyces grey-green and the bracts green. Bracteoles are very small and almost insignificant. Careful pruning will give the plant wide but compact growth, no more than 17 cm when in flower. Unpruned, a flowering bush can grow over 27 cm in height.

Although reasonably hardy, it must be positioned carefully in the garden to avoid competition with larger plants — a rock garden is very suitable. It is also ideal for pot culture.

The plant is a rare but precious find in nurseries; although it is easy to propagate, it is slower growing and quite a number of plants are needed to obtain sufficient cutting material.

Lavandula angustifolia 'Alba'
Growing between 40-60 cm with green-grey foliage and linear-shaped leaves, 'Alba' flowers shortly after *L. angustifolia* ssp. *angustifolia* and about the same time as 'Nana Alba'.

The flower spikes are interrupted and 4-7 cm long. The white corollas, with their grey-green calyces and broad green bracts, have a tendency to change to pale lilac with age. Bracteoles are only 1-2 mm in length.

The plant is sweetly fragrant and has a second sparse flowering period. It propagates reasonably well and requires pruning to keep in shape.

The true 'Alba' was bred in Switzerland in 1623. The name 'Alba' has unfortunately led to some confusion in nurseries. *L.* x *intermedia* 'Alba' is often labelled incorrectly as *L. angustifolia* 'Alba'.

Pink-flowering cultivars
Lavandula angustifolia 'Rosea'
(syn. 'Nana Rosea')
Known by its common name of pink lavender, 'Rosea' was introduced prior to 1937, and is a most attractive plant growing 40-60 cm when in flower. The very green foliage is a distinguishing characteristic during the winter months.

Young plants are easy to propagate, vigorous growing and of upright habit. Pruning is required to keep plants compact.

This is one of the earliest-flowering lavenders. The colour of the individual flowers is, in fact, mauve but the corollas appear pink to the naked eye. The calyces are green with plum-coloured stripes, bracts are green and small (1 mm) bracteoles may be present. The spikes are frequently interrupted and 3-6 cm long. Flowering continues over the season but not as abundantly as some other cultivars.

'Rosea' makes a marvellous addition to the garden and adds contrast to other cultivars. It is suitable for hedging and is particularly appealing planted alternately with dark-flowered cultivars such as *L. angustifolia* 'Nana Atropurpurea'. The fragrance is sweet and although the spikes can appear 'muddy' in colour when dry, they are enhanced by arranging with other coloured spikes.

Two other pink cultivars — 'Jean Davis' and 'Loddon Pink' — are almost identical with 'Rosea'.

Lavandula angustifolia 'Hidcote Pink'

This plant, raised in England prior to 1958, is very similar to 'Rosea' except that the leaves are narrower and more grey in colour and the corollas are a slightly darker pink.

Lavandula x *intermedia* cultivars

(syn. *L.* x *hybrida*, *L.* x *burnati*, *L.* x *spica-latifolia*, *L.* x *aurigerana*, *L.* x *senneni*, *L.* x *hortensis*, *L.* x *feraudi*, *L.* x *guilloni*, *L.* x *leptostachya*)

The second group of cultivars in the Spica group are definite hybrids between *L. angustifolia* and *L. latifolia*, and because of the known parentage are called *L.* x *intermedia* prior to the cultivar name.

'Lavandin' is a name often used for plants of this cross, particularly in southern France. These cultivars are characteristically intermediate between the two parents with flowering commencing about 3-4 weeks after *L. angustifolia*. The plants are usually vigorous in growth habit reaching over 1 metre when flowering although some of the foliage may reach only 30–50 cm.

A percentage of the peduncles may be branched, especially towards the end of the season, and the flower spikes may be quite large. The bracts are more narrow and awl shaped and bracteoles (1-4 mm) are always present and usually plentiful. The spikes themselves are paler in colour than those of the *L. angustifolia* cultivars. The leaves are broader and the plants usually have a more camphoraceous fragrance.

They produce flower spikes freely and are more often used for cut flower production or for their oil content. They are propagated by cuttings as they are sterile and rarely produce seed.

Lavender, violet and purple-flowering cultivars
L. x *intermedia* 'Seal'

Originally introduced in England in 1955, 'Seal' can easily reach 80 cm and more than 1 metre when flowering. It needs rigorous pruning to keep its green-grey foliage in shape as it is prone to woodiness.

The flower spikes are variable in shape, being more rounded and open in appearance and anywhere between 3.5 and 7 cm long. The corollas are aster-violet, the calyces and bracts green, the peduncles 45 cm long, and a large plant can produce over 1000 spikes in one season. Flowering commences in late December.

The plant produces a low-grade oil but the

THE ESSENTIAL LAVENDER

L. x *intermedia* 'Yuulong'

*L.*x *intermedia* 'Bogong'

L. x *intermedia* 'Grey Lady'

L. x *intermedia* 'Sussex'

PROFUSION OF LAVENDER

L. x *intermedia* 'Scottish Cottage'

L. x *intermedia* 'Old English'

L. x *intermedia* 'Arabian Night'

L. x *intermedia* 'Grey Hedge'

dried heads are excellent for lavender bags, retaining their scent for many years.

Lavandula x *intermedia* 'Super'

A vigorous–growing plant that when mature can be over 1 metre in flower. It is similar in growth form to 'Seal' but the flower spikes are quite different in shape and size, being wedge-shaped and loosely compact. The spikes are 6-9 cm long with pretty violet corollas and lighter calyces and bracts on long, often branched peduncles. The narrow bracteoles are between 2-3 mm. When in full flower the heads lose their attractive shape.

'Super' is one of the first lavandins to flower (about 2-3 weeks after *L. angustifolia*) and continues blooming for a long period. It has one of the sweetest fragrances of the lavandins.

Lavandula x *intermedia* 'Grosso'

'Grosso' was bred in France by a Monsieur Grosso in about 1972. It is a spectacular plant when in flower, very fine leaved when young. Kept pruned, the plants remain compact and produce masses of blooms from late December through to autumn.

The flower spikes are compact and attractive with violet corollas and calyces and bracts tinged with dark violet. The peduncles are frequently branched in three. Bracteoles are 2-3 mm, slightly smaller than other lavandins. The scent is sweet and camphoraceous.

Cuttings tend to be slow growing when small. The plant is resistant to the disease yellow decline (shab) which destroyed many oil-producing crops in southern France.

'Grosso' is the leading producer of lavender oil worldwide. The quality of the oil nevertheless depends on soil type and prevailing weather conditions. The oil quality can also be affected if the plant has to compete with strongly scented plants such as yarrow (*Achillea millefolium*) and pennyroyal (*Mentha pulegium*), or trees such as eucalypts.

Most oil is produced from glands on the calyces and for maximum production the heads are collected when half the flowers on the spike have shrivelled, usually towards the end of the season.

It is also suitable for dried flower production because of its darker heads.

Lavandula x *intermedia* 'Grey Lady'

This is not the true *L. angustifolia* 'Gray Lady' described on page 36. Its growth habit and foliage is much like that of 'Seal' but the spikes have unusual mineral-violet corollas, aconite-violet calyces and mostly green awl-shaped bracts. Bracteoles are 2-3 mm. The spikes themselves are more loosely arranged and variable in shape.

Lavandula x *intermedia* 'Bogong'

(syn. 'Bujong', 'Byjong')

A tall-growing plant, over 1 metre when flowering, with campanula-violet corollas, aconite-violet calyces and green bracts. The spikes are 5-6 cm long and loosely arranged along the stem. Large 2-4 mm bracteoles are present. The peduncles are at least 40 cm long. The foliage is grey-green and requires pruning to keep its shape. Flowering commences about early January.

Lavandula x *intermedia* 'Dilly Dilly'

An attractive smaller-growing New Zealand-bred cultivar. Masses of fairly compact spikes on long peduncles give the plant the appearance of a porcupine. The corollas are similar in colouring to 'Bogong' but the spikes are darker in appearance.

Although most of the peduncles of a young plant are single and unbranched, on older plants branched peduncles do arise with the formation of medium-sized heads on either side of the main stem. Bracteoles (1-3 mm) are present but not as obvious. Flowers appear in late December to early January and have an unusual fragrance.

The plant has sometimes been referred to as *L. angustifolia* 'Dilly Dilly'.

Lavandula x *intermedia* 'Arabian Night'
(syn. 'Arabian Knight', 'Arabian Nights')
Another attractive cultivar selected from the same plant group as 'Dilly Dilly', and very similar in appearance to 'Dilly Dilly'. The heads are quite camphoraceous.

The bracts are awl shaped and the bracteoles narrow and 2-3 mm in length. The plant grows quickly and forms a reasonably compact bush.

Lavandula x *intermedia* 'Sussex'
This New Zealand bred cultivar will readily grow to 45 cm and by its third year can reach over 1 metre when flowering.

The spikes are over 10 cm long and very attractively shaped. The basal portion of the spike is interrupted and 2-3 mm bracteoles are present. The peduncles branch into three.

Lavandula x *intermedia* 'Impress Purple'
This impressive plant produces long branched peduncles and compact spikes of dark violet flowers. It is certainly one of the darkest-flowered lavandin cultivars and with its striking flowerheads is proving to be a great success on the dried flower market.

Lavandula x *intermedia* 'Grappenhall'
(syn. 'Gigantea', 'Giant Grappenhall', 'Grappenhall Variety')
'Grappenhall' was introduced into England at the turn of the century. It is a vigorous plant, growing to 40 cm and up to 80 cm when flowering. The attractive purple spikes are composed of dark lavender-purple corollas with light green calyces suffused with violet. Bracteoles are 1-2 mm long. Flowering commences late December to early January.

Lavandula x *intermedia* 'Wilson's Giant'
A robust cultivar with long peduncles and purple compact spikes which are suitable for floral work. The smell is quite camphoraceous.

The bracts of this cultivar are unusual as they are tinged with bluish purple. The foliage is quite fine when young.

Lavandula x *intermedia* 'Yuulong'
This attractive plant was bred by Yuulong Lavender Estate, Victoria. The plant reaches 65 cm in height and 90 cm when flowering after 3 years' growth. It has long peduncles and 4-5 cm spikes with violet-blue corollas and grey-green calyces. The peduncles become shorter as the plant ages.

It flowers about 2 weeks later than *L. angustifolia*, peaking towards the end of December.

THE ESSENTIAL LAVENDER

L. x intermedia 'Grosso'

L. x intermedia 'Super'

PROFUSION OF LAVENDER

L. x *intermedia* 'Dilly Dilly'

L. x *intermedia* 'Seal'

43

Grey-leaved cultivars

Lavandula x intermedia 'Grey Hedge'

Raised in Britain, this lovely silver-grey-leaved cultivar easily reaches over 1 metre in flower. It has long peduncles and narrow flower spikes of blue-violet corollas and light-coloured calyces and bracts. The bracteoles are 2-3 mm long and 1 mm wide. Flowering is usually in late December to early January.

It is not grown for its fragrance or oil-producing qualities but for its foliage and hedging attributes. When kept well pruned it makes a medium-sized to large hedge.

Lavandula x intermedia 'Scottish Cottage'

Another beautiful grey-leaved cultivar like 'Grey Hedge' and very similar to 'Grey Hedge' in size and shape. The flower spikes are also similar in colour but tend to be slightly broader overall. Flowering may be later than 'Grey Hedge'.

Lavandula x intermedia 'Old English'

(syn. *L. spica*)
A large plant which is over 1 metre when flowering. It was introduced in the 1950s and is similar in growth habit to 'Seal'.

The foliage is grey-green, and not as grey as the other cultivars. The leaves are quite broad. The spikes are similar in appearance to 'Grey Hedge' although the corollas are slightly darker.

Lavandula x intermedia 'Chaix'

This plant is also similar to 'Grey Hedge' but the foliage has a more silver-grey appearance. Although not a prolific flowerer, it is a superb foliage plant. Unfortunately, it is not well known.

White-flowering cultivar

Lavandula x intermedia 'Alba'

A white-flowered lavandin that will grow 60-70 cm tall with peduncles up to 30 cm long on a mature plant. The spikes, produced in early January, are composed of white corollas, grey-green calyces and green bracts slightly tinged with purple. Large (4-5 mm) bracteoles are present and very noticeable. The leaves are broad and the foliage grey-green, sometimes quite grey when young. The fragrance is sweet with camphoraceous overtones.

It can be difficult to propagate and care needs to be taken to ensure that young rooted cuttings are not overwatered. Once the plant is established, the growth rate speeds up and the plants are quite hardy.

This is the variety of white lavender usually sold in nurseries.

INTERSECTIONAL CROSSES

Lavandula x allardii

There is little information on the origin of this plant, commonly known as mitcham lavender. It is thought to be a hybrid between *L. dentata* and *L. latifolia*. It combines this parental mixture by producing grey semi-toothed leaves and growing into a large bush easily exceeding 1 metre in height and width by the time it is 3 years old.

Flower spikes are long and resemble those of the Spica-group lavenders, with dark purple corollas and pale bracts. Bracteoles are also present. The flowerheads are attached to long peduncles which together with the size of the plant create an impressive display. Both the foliage and flowerheads have a mixed camphoraceous and true lavender fragrance.

Although it seems to favour coastal conditions and a sandy soil for maximum growth it will grow in most well-drained soils and is hardy.

The flower spikes can be dried for floral arrangements but are not always suitable for fresh displays as they have a tendency to droop.

The plant makes a wonderful focal point or background border plant in the garden. It is also suitable for hedging providing it is kept in shape with appropriate pruning.

L. x *heterophylla*

This may also be a cross between *L. latifolia* and *L. dentata*. Superficially, the plant is very similar to Spica-group lavenders, being of large habit (up to 1 metre) with branched stems. The shape of the flower spike is also similar and very interrupted up the stem. However, the mature basal leaves may be completely or partially toothed similar to *L.* x *allardii*. It has a sweet camphoraceous smell similar to *L.* x *allardii*.

SECTION PTEROSTOECHAS

This group has the largest number of species, three of which are available through select nurseries in Australasia. They are herbaceous plants with much-branched stems and often slightly woody at the base. The species have pinnate or bipinnate leaves but other species in this group can and do have a variety of different leaf shapes.

The name 'pterostoechas' refers to the shape of the flower spikes. When viewed from the side, the corollas have the appearance of wings. The bracts are all fertile and there are no sterile bracts at the top of the spike. Bracteoles are also

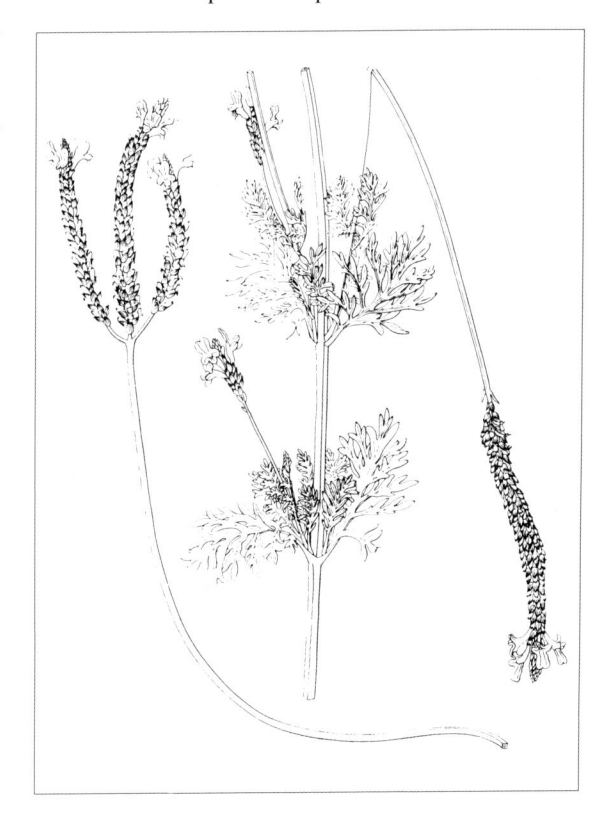

Lavandula multifida (from de Gingins-Lassaraz, Histoire Naturelle des Lavandes, 1826).

L. x allardii *L. x heterophylla*

absent. The flowers do not have the classic 'lavender' fragrance and are grown mainly for interest and as an attractive addition to the garden in warmer climates.

They are native to northern Africa and the Mediterranean region. As such, they are generally not very hardy but in frost-free areas where there is warmth and a little humidity these species will thrive. They can either be grown from seed in spring or propagated from basal cuttings (tip cuttings are often too soft).

Lavandula multifida

In suitable conditions this sub-shrub will grow to 1 metre in height with erect and branched stems covered with soft hairs.

The leaves are green and bipinnate or pinnate, softly fern-like. The flower spikes are 2-7.5 cm in length, often borne singly or branched into three separate heads. The peduncles are usually hairy. The large corollas are a pretty lavender-blue.

It is best grown as a half-hardy perennial, and although it will survive mild frosts it tends to die back to the ground in winter and resume its growth in spring. If well cared for, it will produce flower spikes over most of the summer.

The smell of the foliage is unusual and quite strong — not a lavender fragrance.

Lavandula canariensis

The Canary Islands lavender is an impressive plant to have in your garden with its bright green foliage and long lavender-blue to violet spikes. In suitable conditions it will grow to 1.5 metres with slightly hairy pinnate to bipinnate leaves. The spikes are long and narrow, sometimes up to 10 cm in length and usually branched at the base to form a group of three. The peduncles can be over 45 cm in length.

Unfortunately, it tends to be frost tender and in colder regions is best pot grown so that it can be transferred to the glasshouse for winter.

Lavandula pinnata
A very pretty species with greyish green leaves which are mostly pinnate with broad flat lobes. The whole plant is covered in short hairs.

When fully grown it can reach 1 metre in flower, producing 3-9 cm spikes with blue-purple corollas on long peduncles. The flowerheads, like *L. canariensis*, are often branched into three.

Its foliage has the most pleasant fragrance of the three species mentioned here.

LAVENDER – A GARDENER'S DELIGHT

Among the roses soft in hue
Lie beds of fragrant lavender blue
Awash with violets, pinks and cream
An enchanted setting in which to dream.

AS in centuries past, lavender remains a treasured plant to have growing in the garden for its fragrance and numerous uses. There would be few gardens that are not graced with at least one of these exquisite plants.

Presently lavender is experiencing an even greater resurgence of popularity in the wake of the cottage garden trend of the last 10 years. Yet, whereas previously people would only grow one specimen, today gardeners are planting them *en masse* — as hedging, in knot gardens or as border plants — filling the garden scene with colour and the evening air with their aromatic fragrance. It is a delight to see them also growing in public places, outside shops, petrol stations and even as traffic island centrepieces.

Lavender is generally amenable to most conditions but like many of our garden plants cannot withstand extreme climates.

Of the three groups commonly cultivated, it is only the Spica-group lavenders that do not favour the high humidity experienced in the north of the North Island in New Zealand and in New South Wales and Queensland in Australia. In those regions, the cultivation of Spica lavenders can prove difficult. Nevertheless, there will probably always be someone who can grow lavenders successfully even in the most adverse conditions and there will always be pockets of land in these areas that will prove favourable. Overall, we are very fortunate in having climatic conditions that generally allow a good opportunity to grow lavender.

COMMERCIAL GROWING

Lavenders have long been grown overseas commercially for their oil production — still an essential ingredient in the cosmetic industry. Much of the world's lavender oil is grown and distilled in the south of France and there are well-known lavender farms in England and Jersey. There are also large commercial ventures closer to home. For example, in Australia

Lavandula 'Helmsdale'.

Lavandula 'Avonview'.

<u>Left to right</u>: *L.* x *intermedia* 'Seal' *and L.* x *intermedia* 'Alba'.

we Lavender Estate, Tasmania, has been
ng top-grade lavender oil for many years,
ulong Lavender Estate in Victoria attracts thousands of visitors a year to view lavender and sample lavender products.

In New Zealand the main oil-producing plant used is *L.* x *intermedia* 'Grosso' and much research has been carried out by Crop and Food Research Ltd to discover local optimum oil-producing conditions and areas. Redbank Research Station in Central Otago has proved an ideal location for growing lavenders and research with a number of different cultivars is continuing.

CULTIVATION

Most lavenders are easily grown and require but a few necessities to keep them happy.

A well-drained soil and an abundance of sunlight are the two most important prerequisites when deciding on a site. Providing the soil is free draining, lavenders will adapt to most soil types. They prefer lighter soils and thrive if grown in a good loamy, gritty mix. Poorly drained, heavy clays and a flooded garden will quickly demoralise plants. Water-logged soils can be improved by installing underground drainage pipes or adding compost and humus. Raised beds will also assist with this problem. Other suitable sites are rock gardens, hillsides or surfaces with a run-off.

Lavenders from the Spica group prefer an alkaline soil with a pH of about 6-8; a sprinkling of chalk, lime or superphosphate can be added to raise the pH. Stoechas-group lavenders grow well in most places and in France some even grow in quite acidic soils. The prevalence of *L. stoechas* types in Tasmania and the rural areas of Victoria and the necessity to ban them as noxious plants in these areas of Australia indicates that they are reasonably tolerant of soil type.

Many lavenders will seed themselves and grow in crevices in concrete, pots, steps, gravel and even where soil has collected in the bark of trees. When the conditions are right, lavender flourishes.

However, sunlight is vital for lavenders and it is preferable that they receive sun for at least three-quarters of the day. In many situations this is not possible during winter so take this into consideration before planting.

Cold temperature can affect lavenders in the Stoechas and Pterostoechas groups. They thrive in warmer climates and *L. canariensis* and *L. pinnata* are best placed under cover at even a hint of frost. Most of the Stoechas group will survive mild and sometimes quite severe frosts if they have been raised or acclimatised in a colder climate. However, in colder areas plant them where they will be sheltered during winter.

Lavenders that are frost tender will benefit from being grown near buildings that radiate heat during the winter months. For example, roof extensions or eaves can be valuable shelter for plants of the less hardy Pterostoechas group.

The Spica-group lavenders prefer a cool climate during the winter and warm, sunny summers. They are reasonably hardy and will withstand frosts but will not survive where snow lies on the ground for any length of time. Late frosts sometimes reduce flowering potential by damaging flower buds.

Both overwatering and severe drought conditions can also adversely affect growth and flower production.

Stoechas and Pterostoechas groups thrive in warmer, humid conditions but too much humidity can be detrimental to members of the Spica group which under these circumstances can become susceptible to root rot and other diseases. If growing the English lavenders in areas prone to high humidity, choose a site that has at least some air movement and space the plants well apart. An interesting method of reducing fungal attack is to put a layer of white sand or shells to a depth of 3-5 cm around the base of and between the plants. This results in both light and heat being reflected into the centre of the plant, drying the plant out and and reducing the risk of rot or fungal infections. This apparently also stimulates flower production. Combine a little lime and chalk with sand to make up a white mix suitable for this purpose or there may be a source of white golden sand nearby that can be used unadulterated.

Although lavenders will survive windy conditions they grow better in a sheltered position. Where warm, dry winds are prevalent, watch that the plants do not become drought stressed. Such winds will also affect the oil content of the plants.

In dry, warm spring and summer conditions irrigation is essential to encourage overall growth and flower production. However, if conditions are slightly cooler, protect against overwatering as an excess will lead to root and foliage rot.

Consideration needs to be given to spacing when laying out a lavender bed. For example, most lavandins will eventually grow to a metre or more in height when flowering and can often be as wide. Therefore, a distance of a metre between them and other plants would be appropriate if they are to grow into their true form. If they are being used as a hedge then a distance of between 50–75 cm between plants will suffice. The smaller *L. angustifolia* cultivars can be planted anywhere between 30-70 cm apart depending on their growth habit.

Annual and perennial weeds can be a problem and it is always best to prepare the site carefully prior to planting to reduce future problems. Weeds around lavender can be controlled by spraying, mulching, hoeing or hand weeding.

Lavenders in the ground do not generally require fertilisers although a foliar application of nitrogen in the spring may assist growth in young plants and help increase flower production and stem length for dried-flower purposes. The addition of well-rotted compost will enrich the soil and also act as a mulch to suppress weeds.

PESTS AND DISEASES

Very few pests and diseases bother lavenders in Australasia. The spittle bug (*Philaenus spumarius*) is one of the main offenders found on plants. Its presence is easily detected on bushes in spring as small areas of spittle on the plant. If these are cleared away a small, soft green insect will be

THE ESSENTIAL LAVENDER

Left to right: *L. angustifolia* 'Rosea' *and* *L. angustifolia* 'Hidcote'.

Lavandula angustifolia 'Gray Lady'.

Lavandula angustifolia 'Alba'.

found. In the home garden these do not cause much damage and can be removed by frequent hosing, spraying or, if there are only a few, picking them off with a paintbrush into a bucket of water.

Watch seedlings and newly rooted cuttings for caterpillar damage and protect against rabbits which can nibble foliage.

Alfalfa mosaic virus (AMV) is vectored by aphids and causes yellow patches on leaves and occasional twisting of young spring growth, which results in decreased plant vigour. It will not kill the plant but will damage commercial crops, so where it occurs, aphid control needs to be enforced as the disease cannot as yet be eradicated from an affected plant.

Other diseases include lavender leafspot and bacterial blast which are not considered detrimental and can be prevented. Overseas, shab, a fungal disease, can be a major problem but fortunately is not present in Australasia.

PRUNING

Lavenders in the Spica group are best pruned after flowering and well before the cold weather sets in to allow the new growth to 'harden'. Plants in this group respond well to appropriate pruning and the reward is more even foliage growth and an abundance of flowers during the summer flowering season.

Prune old flowerheads from the plant and trim into a dome shape. Observe the plant and discover where the new growth arises so that appropriate action can be taken. For example, if the plant produces new growth from all parts of the plant, like *L. angustifolia* 'Munstead', then a reasonable pruning will produce a compact growth habit. Some plants, however, do not produce new growth uniformly over the plant and need to be cut back reasonably hard to encourage young growth at the base. If a plant with basal growth like this is not well pruned, over time the lower stems will eventually become woody and bare, and the plant will need to be replaced. Occasionally an old plant can be revitalised with careful pruning into the old wood, but again this depends on the habit of the cultivar.

Both the Stoechas-group and Pterostoechas-group lavenders flower more frequently so will need to be pruned during summer.

Members of the Stoechas group can also be trimmed into a rounded shape. They are generally easier to prune because of their abundant growth habit and in warm conditions can be pruned quite low to the ground if required. New growth in summer conditions will be rapid.

Pterostoechas-group lavenders are probably best pruned carefully with secateurs unless you are fortunate to live in an area where they grow prolifically such as New South Wales in Australia and the north of the North Island of New Zealand — if so, hedge-trimmers can be used.

The intergroup cross *L.* x *allardii* can easily withstand pruning to within 15 cm of the ground and will actually benefit from this when the growth has become too 'straggly'.

Very young plants of all types can be carefully pruned into shape with secateurs.

PROPAGATION

Lavenders are generally propagated by cuttings to keep the plants true to type. There are a few exceptions, however. For example, Pterostoechas-group lavenders usually grow true from seed and can sometimes be difficult to grow from cuttings. Keep them separate when flowering to make sure of the seedlings' identity. Most of this group is frost tender and requires either winter protection or re-propagation from seed each spring.

Some of the Stoechas-group plants will also grow true from seed but others will produce an interesting array of hybrids. The majority of lavenders from the Stoechas group are best propagated from cuttings.

Raising plants from seed can result in interesting genetic variation, but a plant so produced cannot always be given its parent's name. Nevertheless, seed collected in the wild, where there are no other lavenders with which to cross-pollinate, will often produce authentic plants.

Lavenders from the Spica group, especially the cultivars, are also best grown from cuttings. However, *L. lanata* and *L. latifolia* will generally grow true from seed providing they have been kept separate from other lavenders in this group.

Cuttings 5-10 cm in length may be taken in spring and autumn and grown either in cold frames or with bottom heat and misting.

Take tip cuttings in spring and tip cuttings or the old-fashioned heel cuttings from semi-hardwood growth in autumn. Adding rooting hormones will aid root formation and accelerate the process.

Root the cuttings in a mixture of soil and sand, soil and perlite or just pure perlite. Vermiculite can be used but breaks down over a period of time. Perlite is probably the best additive as it is very free draining. Coarse river sand or pumice can also be used.

Tissue culture is possible although the plants have to be carefully nurtured once out of the tubes until they are strong enough to survive outdoors. Newly rooted cuttings also need to be carefully watched and must be kept damp (not wet) until they have established themselves. Over-watering can lead to root rot, particularly in young plants. A careful balance must be maintained, however, as desiccation can also be a problem with young plants.

Once the roots have grown through the base of their polythene bag or pot the plants are ready to be transferred either into the ground or into larger pots.

HARVESTING AND DRYING LAVENDER

Choose a dry, sunny day — and harvest the lavender in the mid-morning after the dew has evaporated. Collect only material that is good quality and undamaged.

Lavender heads are best cut when the first two flowers on the spike have opened. They need to be watched carefully as once the first few spikes are ready the remainder will follow within a few days. If left until the spikes have most of their flowers open or are 'fully blown' the dried heads will disintegrate over a period of time, which can be disappointing in a floral arrangement.

Usually the leaves need to be stripped off the stems before drying. Bunches of lavender are then tied together and hung upside down from rafters, cords, nails or something especially made for the purpose. Alternatively, lavender can be dried on muslin trays. Regardless of the method used, lavender must be dried in a darkened environment with plenty of dry air circulation. The location may be a spare bedroom with curtains drawn and the windows open on a sunny day, or a garage or disused shed.

Lavender is dry when the stems break cleanly. Once ready the lavender is best used within a year as the colour fades and, unless the heads are destined for lavender bags or pot-pourri, the scent will also gradually diminish with time.

Nothing destroys dried flowers faster than being stored in the light or a moist environment. As such, when the flowers are dried, store in cupboards or opaque containers in a dry environment.

All lavenders will dry quite well but some are more popular than others because they retain their colour and/or scent better. A dehydrator will produce good results for flowers that are normally difficult to dry. A microwave can also be used.

Of the Stoechas group, flowerheads of *Lavandula dentata* and *L. dentata* var. *candicans* will dry quite well. The heads are best picked as they come into flower and look very attractive in flower arrangements, pot-pourri, floral hats and wall decorations. *Lavandula* 'Helmsdale' with its slightly shorter sterile bracts and rich colour is a good specimen to dry for pot-pourri, wreaths and floral arrangements.

Lavandula stoechas and its subspecies, on the other hand, do not dry as well and are not as popular because of their generally shorter stems. The sterile bracts or 'rabbit's ears' are difficult to dry because of their length although they do press well. If using any of the *L. stoechas* hybrids, pick the flower spikes just as they are coming into full colour.

Most flowerheads in the Spica group dry well and it basically comes down to a matter of personal choice as to which variety you choose.

Experiment and discover which lavenders dry most appropriately for their required use. For example, many lavender spikes are used by themselves and do not require a stem since they can be hot-glued directly into arrangements or on objects to be decorated. Do not discard heads that have broken off during the drying process as they may be of value for small projects.

CONTAINER GROWING

Lavenders adjust well to container growing as long as they have adequate drainage. Most potting mixes are suitable but one made specifically for container growing may be preferable. The soil must be free draining but able to retain water sufficiently to prevent desiccation.

Adequate watering is as important for lavenders as it is for most potted plants. During summer check lavenders every few days because if the roots are allowed to dry the plant could

Lavender drying.

die. If it becomes necessary to water them every day then the plant may need repotting into a larger container. During winter, however, watering is best kept to a minimum so that the plants do not contract root rot. This is important with young plants, which may be better kept under shelter and away from heavy rain.

Some lavenders are more suitable for container growing than others. These are generally the smaller-growing and medium-sized *L. angustifolia* cultivars such as 'Nana Alba', 'Munstead', and 'Blue Mountain', and the pink cultivars which grow well from the base. Other cultivars from this group can also be pot grown but will require more pruning to keep in shape.

<u>Opposite above</u>: *A mature specimen of L. lanata.*
<u>Opposite, left</u>: *Lavandula stoechas ssp. stoechas 'Alba' in the large pot, L. angustifolia 'Munstead' behind on right, L. angustifolia 'Folgate' behind on left.*
<u>Opposite, right</u>: *L. angustifolia 'Nana Alba' with L. angustifolia 'Munstead'.*

Lavandins, being generally larger-growing plants, are not often suitable for pot culture. However, they can be grown this way for the first few years of their life and can create a charming display in large jardinieres. After 2 years they have usually grown too large to be enclosed and will need to be planted in the garden.

Any of the grey-leaved lavandin cultivars are effective in pots and *L.* x *intermedia* 'Impress

LAVENDER — A GARDENER'S DELIGHT

57

Purple' and 'Grosso', with their darker flower heads and compact growth, are also suitable.

Container-grown lavenders should be carefully root and foliage pruned to maintain their shape but this can be time-consuming and it may be more convenient to grow the smaller lavenders in wide-mouthed containers and plant the larger ones in the garden.

All container-grown lavenders will need to be repotted at least once a year in early spring. Sometimes you may need to do this in autumn as well, as in optimum conditions lavender roots will tend to spread quickly. A general fertiliser may need to be added at regular intervals during the growing season.

HEDGES

A small lavender hedge gives form to pathways and confers a sense of enclosure and peace to a landscape while outlining flowerbeds and structures as important garden features. A hedge can lead the eye to a focal point or simply an arresting feature in itself. They can be curved and shaped to suit any particular need.

Small- and medium-sized lavender hedges can be used to frame paths or form knot gardens or outline garden ornaments and statues. Larger hedges can be used to partition areas or outline enclosures.

Most lavenders from the Spica group and some from the Stoechas group make suitable hedges. *Lavandula angustifolia* 'Munstead' has been traditionally used as a small- to medium-sized hedging plant, growing quickly and recovering well after pruning; *L. angustifolia* 'Blue Mountain', with its compact grey foliage and attractive flowerheads, also lends itself to hedging. *Lavandula angustifolia* ssp. *angustifolia*, *L. angustifolia* 'Irene Doyle' and the pink-flowered cultivars will produce medium-sized hedges, and *L. angustifolia* 'Avice Hill' is a good form for attracting the attention to garden ornaments such as bird baths or sun dials. Any of the *L. angustifolia* cultivars that grow well from the base following pruning will make effective hedges.

Lavandula angustifolia 'Nana Atropurpurea' and *L. angustifolia* 'Rosea' look particularly attractive together. Try planting these alternately in a circular shape to create a splash of purple, and pink. *L. angustifolia* 'Alba' could be added to provide a white variation.

Try *L. angustifolia* 'Twickel Purple' as a medium to large hedge but it will need to be kept well trimmed as it has a tendency to sprawl when in flower.

Lavandins can be used to create larger hedges, some of which can be over 1 metre when flowering. The most commonly used lavender in this group is *L.* x *intermedia* 'Grey Hedge' with its abundant strongly growing grey foliage. It can be pruned hard to make a smaller hedge but is far more spectacular when allowed to grow to a larger size and will still form a compact shape when kept to 70 cm.

Of the other lavandins, *L.* x *intermedia* 'Scottish Cottage' also makes a suitable hedge. The beautiful grey leaves of these plants make a wonderful background for other plants in the garden. *L.* x *intermedia* 'Impress Purple' and

'Grosso', with their compact growth and lovely darker violet flowerheads, could also be used for medium-sized hedges. However, *L.* x *intermedia* 'Grosso' tends to be slow growing when young so bear this in mind when planning a hedge.

Many of the Stoechas group can be used for hedging, including *L. viridis*, *L. stoechas* ssp. *stoechas* and the hybrids. *Lavandula stoechas* ssp. *stoechas* makes the smallest hedge in this group and forms a very attractive compact display that flowers for long periods. *Lavandula dentata* and *L. dentata* var. *candicans* make wonderful large-growing hedges in warmer areas. The latter will easily reach 1.5 metres in optimum conditions and looks marvellous as a boundary fence or leading to an entranceway of a garden or house.

One factor that is important when growing a lavender hedge is pruning. Insufficient pruning as a hedge is forming will result in 'leggy' plants over time which means that the hedge will need to be replaced sooner. This is particularly true for plants such as *L.* x *intermedia* 'Grey Hedge' and 'Scottish Cottage'. Cut plants back so that the new growth is being produced from the base. This principle applies to many hedging plants — maintenance commences before the hedge is formed.

Hedges usually need trimming twice a year. Be careful not to prune flower buds and allow sufficient time before cold weather sets in.

Spacing between plants is usually best determined by noting the width of a mature plant and plant half that distance apart.

KNOT GARDENS

*'The knotte garden serveth for pleasure
The potte garden for profitte'*

During Elizabethan times knot gardens, parterres and arbours were popular features in English gardens, and even today they still elicit a response of delight.

Traditionally, a knot garden is one composed of hedges or 'threads' which are continuous, having no beginning and no end. The hedges were traditionally composed of either one or a mixture of the following: lavender, santolina (e.g. *Santolina chamaecyparissus*), marjoram (*Origanum vulgare*), sage (*Salvia officinalis*), rosemary (*Rosmarinus officinalis* 'Tuscan Blue'), hyssop (*Hyssopus officinalis*), wall germander (*Teucrium chamaedrys*), roman chamomile (*Anthemis nobilis*), pennyroyal (*Mentha pulegium*), winter savory (*Satureja montana*), thyme (*Thymus vulgaris, T. fragrantissimus*), southernwood (*Artemisia abrotanum*) or box (*Buxus sempervirens*). Knot gardens were divided into two types. Where the hedges or threads were interwoven into an intricate design, the creation was said to be a 'closed knot'. The interlacing threads were usually made of different plants to distinguish how the threads wove in and out, over and under.

In 'open knot' gardens, on the other hand, the threads did not interlace and one was free to walk into the garden.

If space was available to make a large knot garden, the area was divided into four sections, each one of different design. The border of each of these sections was surrounded with 'taller or

Above: Here an ornate bird bath forms a focal point in the garden. Lavandula x. intermedia 'Seal' is in the right foreground. From left front: *L. stoechas* ssp. *caesia, L. x. intermedia* 'Grey Hedge', *L. stoechas* ssp. *stoechas* 'Alba', *and L. dentata* var. *candicans*. Behind the statue is *L. viridis* and *L. angustifolia* 'Munstead'.
Left: A small garden statue fringed by *L. dentata*.
Opposite: A small courtyard has been transformed into a knot garden. Lavandula 'Helmsdale' is contained by Buxus hedging and 'Iceberg' roses provide the floral display. Four robinias give height to the garden.

thicker herbs than those used in the centre'. The hedges surrounding the knot gardens could be topiaried to add further appeal.

Traditionally, closed knot gardens had the spaces between their threads filled with coloured

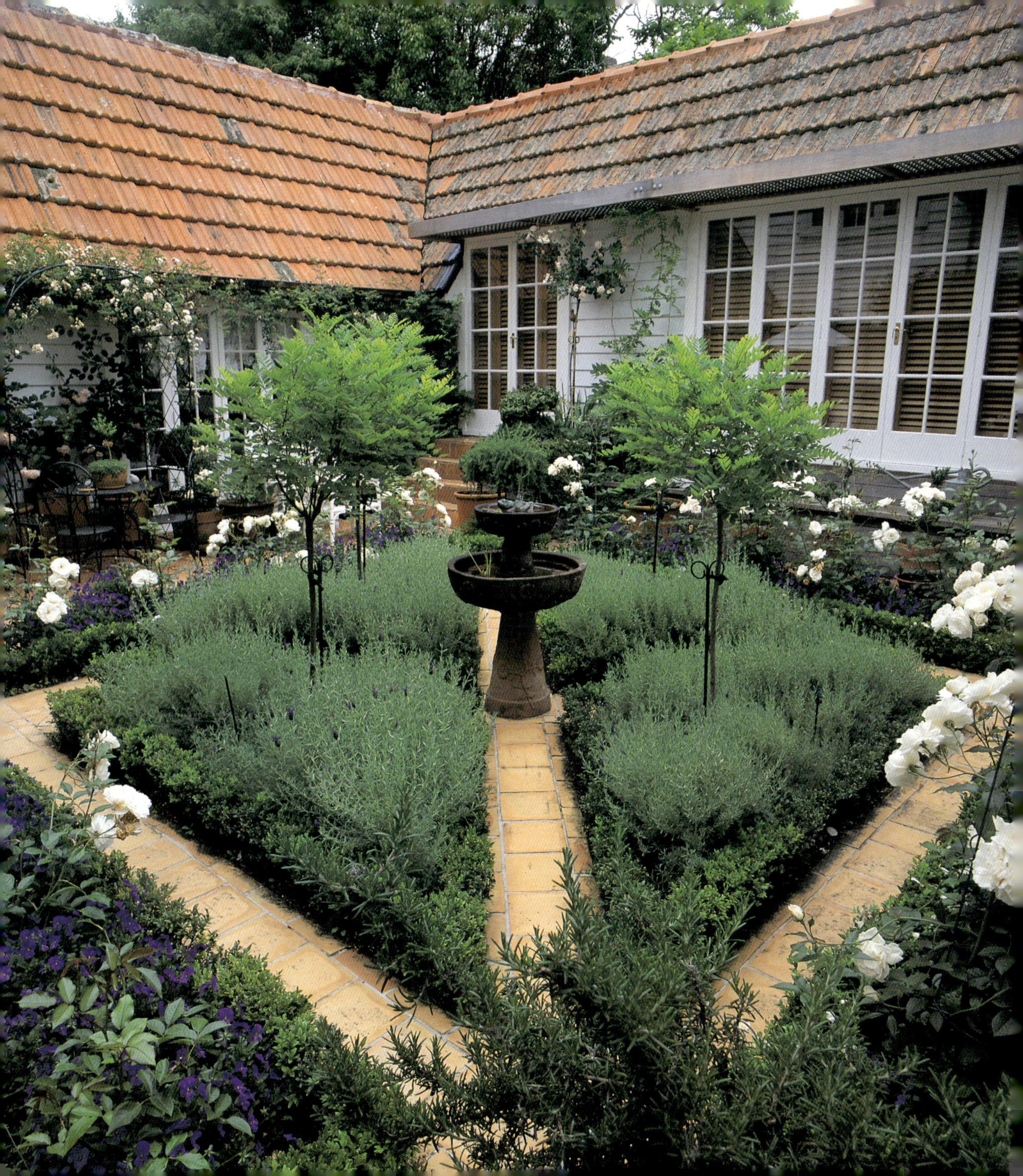

soil with the heraldic colours predominating. To make these coloured soils the following methods can be used: black soils, deep black loam; red soils, broken and crushed red bricks; yellow soils, yellow clay or yellow/golden sand; white soils, limechalk dust; and blue soils, mixed chalk and coal dust together.

The enclosures outlined by an open knot garden were filled with smaller plants and occasionally with topiaried specimens. Bulbs were also used to create a spring-flowering effect.

A knot garden would certainly look impressive as a large full-scale design on the front lawn but this is often not appropriate with today's small suburban sections. However, miniature knot gardens can make an appealing alternative and are equally intriguing to design and lay out.

Inspiration for knot gardens can be found everywhere — from ceiling designs and patterns on furniture and vinyl floors to mandalas. If you want to use a sixteenth-century design, refer to *The Gardener's Labyrinth* by Thomas Hyll which was written during the Elizabethan period.

Composing and then planting one's own design can be a very satisfying achievement. One year a friend of mine decided to create a knot garden in the form of a butterfly. The shape was drawn out proportionally on graph paper and a site chosen. The soil was carefully prepared to a fine tilth and raked over. Then armed with ruler, markers and string we proceeded to map the overall framework. The shape of the wings was first measured out and marked with small white pegs so that the overall proportions could be

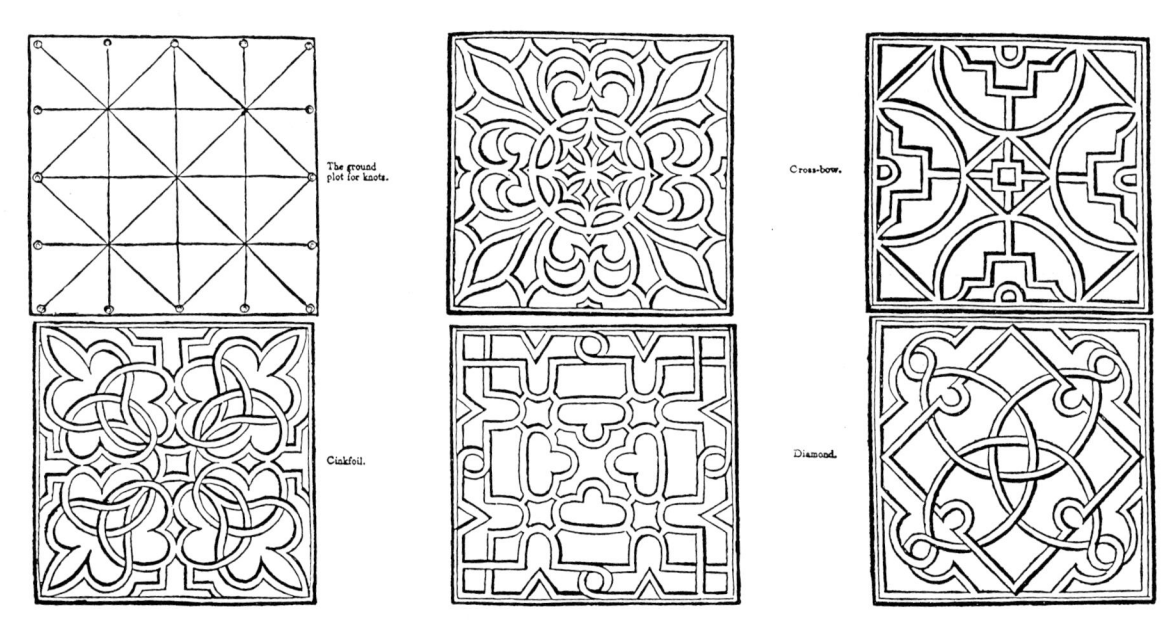

Jacobean knot-garden designs (from William Lawson, The Country House-Wifes Garden, *1653)*

checked before planting commenced. The head and thorax were composed of stones and the abdomen was shaped by small flat stones with lawn chamomile (*Anthemis nobilis* 'Treneague') as a filler. The wings were outlined with hedges of lavender and different coloured thymes (*Thymus*) and the interior of the wings filled with thrift (*Armeria maritima*), *Allium*, dwarf white lavender, golden marjoram (*Origanum vulgare* 'Aureum'), *Silene* and calamint (*Calamintha grandiflora*). Hedge hyssop (*Gratiola officinalis*) was planted for antennae.

A very simple miniature knot garden can be planted in the shape of a square using *L. angustifolia* 'Munstead'. The interior can have a simple pattern woven in winter savory (*Satureja montana*) and common thyme (*Thymus vulgaris*).

One of the most important points to remember when making a knot garden is the site. Preferably choose one that can be viewed from an upstairs window, but if this is not possible then position the garden so it can be seen to best advantage from the house. Prepare the ground and mark out your design as described for the butterfly garden using pegs and strings. Another method for adding the final lines of the design between markers is to use sand.

Lavenders suitable for knot-garden hedging must be the small-growing varieties with abundant growth from the base. Plants that develop woody trunks are not suitable. *L. angustifolia* 'Munstead' has traditionally been used as a 'knot garden thread' but other suitable plants worth trying are *L. angustifolia* ssp. *angustifolia*, *L. angustifolia* 'Irene Doyle', and 'Avice Hill'. Of the dark-flowered cultivars *L. angustifolia* 'Blue Mountain' would probably be the best for knot garden hedging; the others could be used but would need to be well cut back.

The taller-flowering stems of the lavandin group may appear incongruous in a knot garden design and many tend to grow too vigorously for this type of hedging.

Knot garden hedging must be kept well clipped at all times to maintain its shape.

PLANT ASSOCIATIONS

In a garden setting lavender can blend into the background or display itself boldly as a centrepiece. Planted *en masse*, lavender in bloom is an awe-inspiring sight and delights the senses in every way. In a formal planting or as part of a knot garden border it is no less appealing and topiaried *L. dentata* can add a focal point to any setting. Lavender is also usually present in cottage gardens adding its fragrance, colour and charm to its surrounding neighbours.

Colours change with the light and the time of day. Grey-foliaged plants are more noticeable in the evening light, when white becomes quite luminescent, and red colours are softer, and blue tones more apparent. So sitting on a patio or deck during a summer evening surrounded by lavenders can be an exquisite experience.

The grey-green foliage of most lavenders will act as a foil for other plants in the garden and will greatly enhance colours around it.

Plants with yellow foliage or yellow flowers planted around lavender can add vibrance to a

Above: Circular hedging using *L. angustifolia* 'Rosea' and *L. angustifolia* 'Nana Atropurpurea' *with L. angustifola* 'Hidcote' *to the right and L. angustifolia* ssp. *angustifolia immediately behind and to the right.*
Left: Lavandula dentata *and* 'Iceberg' *roses.*
Opposite: Here lavender is the hedging, framing beds of Nepeta 'Six Hills Giant' and lavatera.
Below: One of the most colourful companions for lavender is Santolina virens, here companioned with L. x intermedia 'Super'.

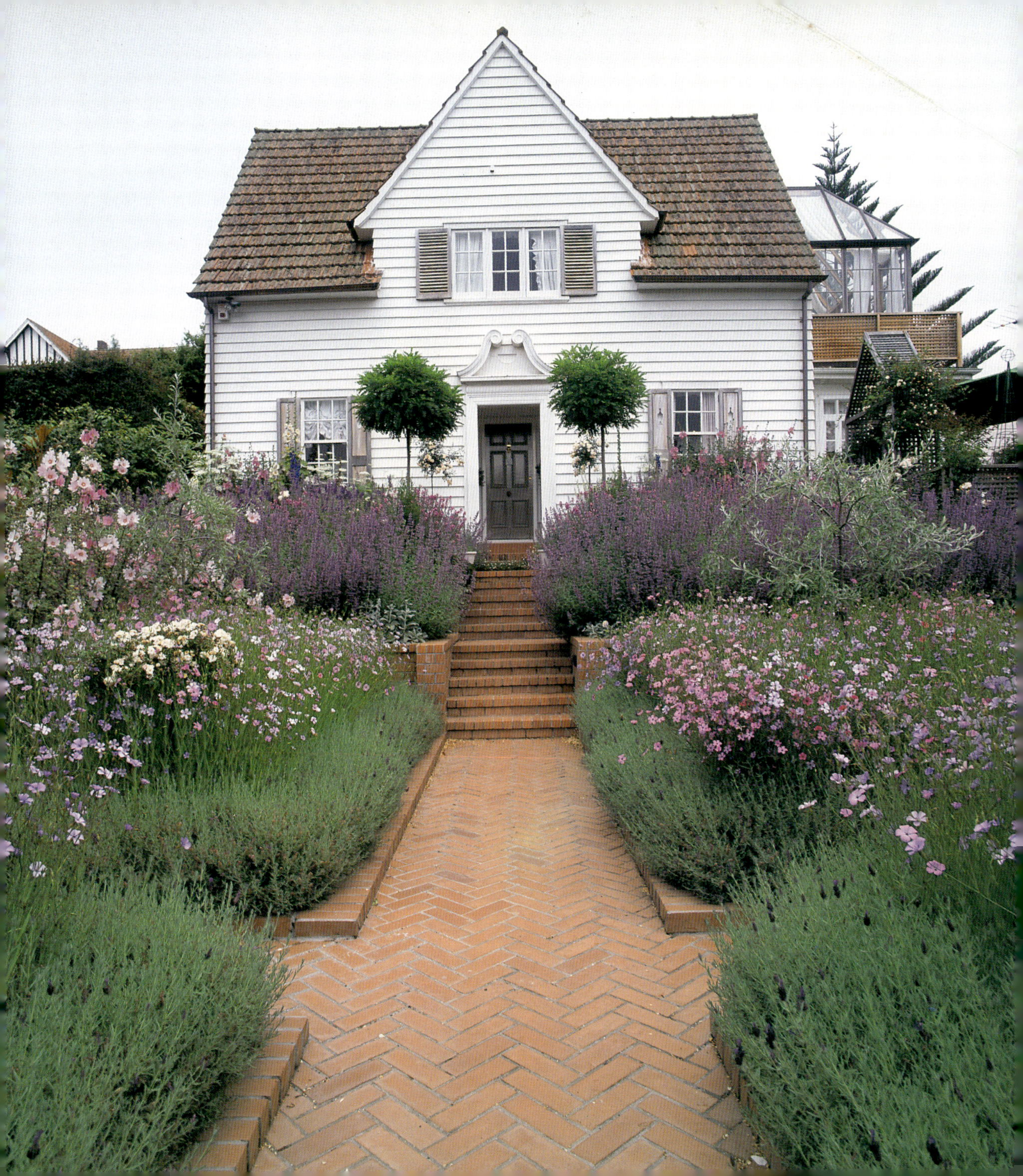

garden and yellow is a colour that remains bright in the evening light. For example, any of the grey-leaved lavandins, or *L. angustifolia* cultivars with grey-leaved foliage such as *L. angustifolia* 'Nana Atropurpurea', 'Blue Mountain' and 'Gray Lady' can be planted with lady's mantle (*Alchemilla vulgaris* or *A. mollis*), golden marjoram (*Origanum vulgare* 'Aureum'), golden lemon thyme (*Thymus* x *citriodorus* 'Aureus'), lady's bedstraw (*Galium verum*), sunflowers (*Helianthus annuus*) and yellow coreopsis (*Coreopsis*). The more greenish grey-foliaged lavenders can also be used in this combination for a stronger contrast.

Yellow, scarlet and orange nasturtiums (*Tropaeolum*) and red, pink and purple phlox (*Phlox*) planted together with *L.* 'Helmsdale', 'Marshwood', or any of the dark-flowered *L. angustifolia* cultivars, can create quite a bold summertime display of colour.

Lavenders planted with *Petunia*, snapdragons (*Antirrhinum majus*), *Cosmos*, *Echinacea purpurea*, *Achillea*, red sage (*Salvia officinalis* 'Purpurescens'), other ornamental sages (*Salvia*) and *Campanula* will add colour to the garden.

A particularly striking combination is lavender planted with hollyhocks (*Althaea*) and the true hardy geraniums with their pink, white and lavender-blue flowers. Suitable geraniums include *Geranium sanguineum* with its lobed leaves and pink flowers; *G. grandiflorum* 'Plenum' with its double, purple-blue flowers; *G. renardii* with its rounded grey-green leaves and white flowers with purple veining; and *G. psilostemon* which has spectacular magenta flowers with black centres. Lavenders from both the Stoechas and Spica groups grow well in this combination.

When choosing plants to grow with lavenders it is sometimes best to select those that like high sunlight hours and will survive the occasional dry conditions. If the site chosen is in a particularly warm position, a grey and silver garden can be created by combining plants such as *Stachys lanata*, *Santolina chamaecyparissus*, *Santolina neopolitana*, and smaller-growing grey-leaved artemisias such as *Artemisia schmidtiana* 'Nana' and *A. stelleriana* with lavenders from the Spica group. There are many other plants that can be added to this list and the results are well worth the effort of searching them out.

Ornamental grasses can sometimes add a dramatic touch when planted with lavenders. For example, a grey-foliage grass such as *Festuca glauca* adds to the attraction of the smaller-growing lavenders from the Spica group. Likewise, the ornamental grass *Pennisetum setaceum*, with its long plumed spikes of purplish flowers, blends well with the taller lavandins or with *L.* x *allardii*.

Foxgloves (*Digitalis*) and herbs such as hyssop (*Hyssopus officinalis*), valerian (*Valeriana officinalis*), calamint (*Calamintha officinalis* or the more commonly available *C. grandiflora*), anise hyssop (*Agastache anethiodora*), *Artemisia*, meadowsweet (*Filipendula ulmaria*), liquorice (*Glycyrrhiza glabra*), musk mallow (*Malva moschata*), *Lobelia syphilitica*, lungwort (*Pulmonaria officinalis*), wood betony (*Stachys officinalis*), chicory (*Cichorium intybus*), winter savory (*Satureja montana*), wall germander (*Teucrium chamaedrys*), lemon thyme (*Thymus* x *citriodorus*), orange thyme (*T. fragrantissimus*) and vervain (*Verbena officinalis*) in combination with any of the lavenders create a colourful and fragrant display.

Many other herbs are also suitable to grow with lavender including taller specimens such as the vibrant and aromatic bergamot cultivars (*Monarda*), the beautiful felty leaved marsh mallow (*Althaea officinalis*) with its soft pink blooms, and common myrtle (*Myrtus communis*) with its sweet-smelling foliage.

In warmer climates lavenders can be situated alongside fragrant-leaved pelargoniums such as the lemon-scented *Pelargonium crispum*, the fragrant lemon-rose-scented *P.* 'Rober's Lemon Rose', the lime-scented *P. nervosum*, the peppermint-scented *P. tomentosum* and the many other pelargonium varieties that are available. The leaves of these plants are then available to dry for use in pot-pourris and scented bags alongside dried lavender.

For ground covers around lavender try growing violets (especially *Viola odorata*), ground ivy (*Glechoma hederacea*), cowslips (*Primula veris*), lawn chamomile (*Anthemis nobilis* 'Treneague'), carpeting thymes (*Thymus*) and *Alyssum*.

Other plants that blend well with lavender, either separately or in combination, are: *Lychnis*, in particular *L. coronaria*, *L. flos-jovis* and *L. viscaria* with their attractive flowers of pinks, reds, oranges and scarlets; the different coloured toadflaxes (*Linaria*); *Nepeta* such as *N. x faassenii* or *N.* 'Six Hills Giant'; rosemary (*Rosmarinus*); *Heuchera* 'Palace Purple'; phacelia (*Phacelia tanacetifolia*) with plenty of space between plants; *Veronica* and *Verbena*; statice (*Limonium*), plus other dried flower varieties such as *Helipterum*, *Helichrysum*; *Gypsophila* such as *G. repens* and *G. paniculata* 'Rosy Veil'; and *Delphinium*.

One of the best known associations is with roses. Lavender has a place with all of the rose categories but is probably most happily mixed with the old roses, intermingling its own fragrance as they bloom prior to Christmas. Some old roses worth including in the garden are the damask rose (*Rosa damascena*), *R.* 'Souvenir de la Malmaison' (double, flesh to pale pink flowers)'; 'Cardinal de Richelieu' (double, rich violet-purple flowers); 'Comte de Chambord' (double, rich pink to lilac flowers; 'Salet' (double pink flowers); and the delightful smaller-growing apothecary's rose *R. gallica* 'Officinalis' (semi-double, crimson flowers). Lavenders can be stunning when planted around white-flowered roses such as the floribunda 'Iceberg' or under climbers such as the species Banksia rose, *R. banksiae*, with its scented white flowers.

Lavenders can be grown *en masse* with appropriate spacing and cultivation which creates a landscape in itself. Alternatively, base a design for a lavender garden on the shade and colour of the flower spikes so that a graded sequence is established. Lavenders from the Spica group may be more appropriate for this type of design but do not exclude *L. stoechas* hybrids.

Although it is best to choose lavenders that grow to a similar size when mature, careful pruning can keep all the lavenders uniform. Determine whether the lighter-shade flowers are to be towards the centre and the darker outside or vice versa. Darker shades in the centre will draw the eye to the core and lighter colours in the middle will make the circle appear larger. A mixture of different shades can also be tried.

CREATIVE IDEAS WITH LAVENDER

'If you could have only one oil, let it be lavender!'
— DAVID HOFFMAN, *Herbal Stress Control*

As well as being an attractive ornamental plant in the garden, lavender has many versatile applications. These extend from traditional medicinal and aromatic remedies to culinary recipes, household helpers, and ways in which lavender can be used to beautify your house.

NOTE: The reader's discretion is advised when using lavender as a medicinal remedy. If in doubt, seek the advice of a medical practitioner.

SOOTHING COMFORTS

Uses of lavender essential oil

Lavender has long enjoyed a reputation for its soothing qualities, and in historical literature has been used to alleviate everything from headache to mental illness. One remedy for migraine, for example, consists of a couple of drops of lavender oil placed on an ice cube and sucked slowly. Massaging the temple with lavender oil can also soothe the pain, and if added to a base oil can be used to massage and ease the neck muscles. Combine 1 part lavender oil with 6 parts massage oil to relax the body, relieve muscular tension and dispel anxieties.

Lavender oil can be used undiluted on burns, with repeat applications several times a day. Lavender oil can also reputedly benefit wounds, leg ulcers, eczema, nappy rash, boils, dermatitis, herpes, stretchmarks, bee and wasp stings, rheumatic and muscular pain, lumbago, yeast infections, acne, dry skin and can act as a skin rejuvenator. Mixed with St John's wort oil, it will ease sunburn and has been known to ease ear ache. Diluted with a little olive or safflower oil and rubbed on the skin, lavender oil is useful as an insect repellent.

When added to shampoos or conditioners, lavender oil is said to be beneficial in reducing hair loss and alleviating dandruff.

Lavender oil is a popular choice in aromatherapy and combines well with most other oils except rosemary.

CREATIVE IDEAS WITH LAVENDER

Lavender oil for medicinal comforts — see page 70.

Homemade lavender oil

Half fill a bottle or jar with fresh lavender spikes and cover with olive oil and 1 tablespoon of white vinegar. Leave this mixture on a window sill in the sun for at least 14 days, shaking the bottle at least once a day. At the end of this time, check whether the lavender scent is strong enough for your liking; if not, strain off the flowers, add new ones and repeat the process. Once made, the old flowers can be removed and a couple of new ones added for decoration.

This oil does not replace the more expensive essential lavender oil but is nevertheless an effective substitute for scented bath oil. It can also be used as a salad oil or rubbed on as an insect repellent.

Use a sweetly scented lavender for making the oil. *Lavandula angustifolia*, *L. angustifolia* 'Munstead', *L.* x *intermedia* 'Super' and 'Grosso' are particularly good varieties for perfuming.

Sleep pillow

25 g dried lavender
12 g dried lemon verbena
12 g dried lemon thyme
12 g dried sweet woodruff

A useful traditional remedy for insomniacs is the 'sleep pillow' — a sachet of selected herbs placed in a pillow.

For each pillow cut out two 9 x 9 cm squares of organdie, muslin, cotton or silk. Place the sides together and machine around three sides, allowing 2-cm seams. Fill with dried lavender or the mixture above. Hand-sew along the remaining side and embroider a small motif in the centre of the bag, making sure that both layers of fabric are caught. This allows for an even distribution of dried material. Place the bag inside a pillow.

These scented bags can also be used in lingerie drawers or linen cupboards.

Lavender and honey gargle

3 drops lavender oil
1 teaspoon honey
½ cup boiling water

Mix the ingredients together and add enough cold water to make a warm mixture. Use as a refreshing gargle or mouthwash to allay a sore throat or mouth infection.

HOUSEHOLD HELPERS

Lavender cleansers

Lavender water or lavender vinegar (*see* page 71) can be used for general cleaning purposes. A mixture of 4 tablespoons of lavender oil added to 2 litres of warm water can also be used as an antiseptic cleanser. A bowl of warm water with a little lavender vinegar is suitable for freshening or wiping down a room where someone has been ill.

To create a refreshing atmosphere, especially where there are patients present, gently simmer dried or fresh lavender in a pot of water.

Lavender furniture oil and polish

4 large handfuls lavender flowers
450 ml turpentine
450 ml linseed oil
450 g (approximately) beeswax

Place the lavender flowers and oil together in a double boiler and simmer slowly until the flowers have released their oil. Strain and return to the heat. Add the turpentine and beeswax and pour the mixture into a container before it cools.

Add the beeswax slowly and test a little on a saucer to see if it sets. This makes it easier to regulate the consistency of the polish.

Two teaspoons of lavender oil can also be added to a commercially made furniture cream or polish to add a shine to furniture surfaces. Alternatively, mix a few drops of lavender oil with almond oil to wipe wooden surfaces that are unsuitable for cleaning with disinfectant.

Lavender and sweet cicely water

2 teaspoons cinnamon
1 nutmeg, grated
2 tablespoons dried lavender
1 tablespoon dried sweet cicely
1 litre brandy

Mix the ingredients together in a jar with a non-metalic lid and leave in a warm place for 14 days, then strain into a clean jar or bottle and seal.

This remedy can be used as a compress on a brow to cool a feverish person or as a general cleanser to wipe surfaces.

Insect repellent

6 cups dried lavender
1 cup dried mint
½ cup dried santolina
½ cup ground cloves
½ cup orris root
dried orange or lemon peel

Mix all the ingredients together and use in bags to deter moths from clothes and linen.

CULINARY DELIGHTS

Lavender vinegar

Use white vinegar, wine vinegar, white wine vinegar or cider vinegar for this recipe. Place fresh lavender flowers in a bottle and cover with vinegar — the way you would when making lavender oil. Place the bottle in sunlight and shake thoroughly at least once a day. When the vinegar has turned a lavender-rose colour, strain off the flowers and keep the remaining vinegar. You can also add fresh lavender, other herbs or flowers to the vinegar as an added attraction.

Lavender vinegar can be used in salad dressings, as a hair rinse and for general cleaning and antiseptic purposes. It is also suitable to use on bruises to reduce swelling.

Lavenders from the Spica group are now generally used for making vinegar. You can also make lavender vinegar from *L. stoechas*, as they did in Roman times.

Lavender sugar

This is a simple and inexpensive way of flavouring either white granulated sugar or icing sugar. Place sugar and lightly bruised lavender flowers in a tightly sealed container and leave at least 8 days before using. Another method is to steep lavender flowers in a brown sugar syrup and when this mixture cools and hardens grind it into a powder to flavour desserts.

Alternatively, icing sugar can be perfumed with lavender and mixed with a little lemon juice to make a suitable icing for biscuits and cakes.

Lavender tea (tisane)

Lavender tea is traditionally made using *L. angustifolia* ssp. *angustifolia* — other species contain different essential oils and may be unpleasant if consumed.

Add boiling water to 2 or 3 lavender flowerheads and leave for 4 minutes. It is best to use a pottery or glass container for making the infusion. Add honey if a sweetener is required.

Drinking lavender tisane is particularly helpful in relieving extreme fatigue and physical exhaustion.

A variation to this recipe is to add a few lime flowers to the lavender when infusing the tea.

Lavender as an insect repellent for clothes and linen — see page 71.

Lavender candles — see page 78.

Lavender and apple jelly

Cook 2 kg unripe, chopped apples, and ½ cup lavender flowers in enough water to cover. When the apples are cooked, strain overnight through a jelly bag. Then add 1 cup of sugar per cup of liquid, bring to the boil and keep boiling until the jelly is ready to set. Pour the jelly into sterilised jars and seal tightly.

FRAGRANT GIFTS

Lavender bag
*cotton, organdie, silk or muslin
dried lavender*

Cut a 7 x 12 cm rectangle of material. Machine along the sides and across the bottom. Tidy the fabric with pinking shears. Fill with dried lavender to within 4 cm of the top and tie with a bow.

Spicy lavender mixture for sachets and bags
*50 g dried lavender
25 g each dried thyme, mint and marjoram
25 g dried rose petals
2 g orris root powder
12 g ground cloves (or cinnamon or coriander seed)*

Add the mixture to sachets and bags to make a fragrant posy.

Lavender fans
*cotton, organdie, silk or muslin
dried lavender heads and stems
ribbon*

Cut two pieces of fabric to the shape of a fan and machine around the top and the sides. Trim with pinking shears to neaten. Machine vertical lines of stitching wide enough apart to insert the lavender heads. Leave the stalks showing about 8-10 cm below the fabric. Tie the stalks and the fabric at the bottom of the fan with a length of ribbon.

Lavender accessories — see page 78.

Dry pot-pourri mixture

1 litre dried red rose petals
1 litre dried lavender
½ litre dried hydrangea flowers (different colours)
1 cup dried rose buds
4 tablespoons orris root powder
1 tablespoon ground cloves
1 tablespoon cinnamon stick (ground)
2 drops rose oil
2 drops bergamot oil

Mix the dried petals, buds and flowers together in a large ceramic bowl. Add the orris root and stir by hand, then add the cloves and cinnamon. Add the oils one drop at a time — the actual quantity will depend on personal taste.

Once made, dry pot-pourris are best if stored in glass jars in a dark cupboard for 6-12 weeks before using. This allows the scents to merge. They are, however, made more for their colour appeal and the scent will fade quickly compared with a moist pot-pourri.

Moist pot-pourri mixture

1 litre rose petals (scented)

Partially dry rose petals until they are leathery (about 8 hours). Place them in a crock with a sealed lid. To each 2 cups of packed petals add ¼ cup of iodine-free salt. Press this layer down, add another layer of petals, a layer of salt and so on until the crock is full. The mixture can be added to throughout the flowering season.

Use a potato masher for compressing the layers and once the crock is full a plate with a weight on top is sufficient to keep the petals and salt layers compacted. At times the mixture may smell rather raw and froth a little but this will pass.

When the crock is full, the rose petal mixture must be left for at least 2 months to 'cure' before mixing the other ingredients.

The following flowers can be added to the rose mixture in the same manner as the rose petals or they can be dried separately and added when the rose petals are ready:

1 litre dried lavender
½ litre dried mock orange flowers or rosemary leaves
½ litre dried jasmine flowers or lilac flowers

Break up the rose mixture and mix in the flowers. To every 4 cups of this loose mixture add ¼ cup orris root powder or gum benzoin and add the following spices and herbs:

1 tablespoon crushed cloves
1 tablespoon ground cinnamon stick
1 tablespoon sweet marjoram (optional)
2 teaspoons allspice
1 vanilla pod, finely chopped (optional)

Now add the following oils a couple of drops at a time:

6-10 drops rose oil
6 drops bergamot oil or geranium oil
5 drops jasmine oil
4 drops lemon verbena oil

When the pot-pourri is made, store in airtight

containers for up to 3 months, stirring occasionally. If made and stored carefully this mixture can retain its scent indefinitely. To restore an old mixture, add a little brandy.

The salt will bleach the colour of the flower material, so traditionally moist pot-pourris are kept in closed containers with a sealed lid and opened when the fragrance is to be released. A suitable container would be one with two lids: one being porous and one for containing the scent when not in use. If the pot-pourri is to be displayed, brightly coloured dried flowers can be added in the final mix. However, remember the salt will eventually bleach the dried flowers as well.

Lavender soap

plain, unscented soap
lavender water
lavender oil
ground lavender heads
rolled oats
orris root powder

This is a simple way of making one's own lavender soap.

Grate the unscented soap into a crockery bowl. Soften the soap with enough lavender water to moisten and mix in some drops of lavender oil, ground lavender flowerheads and a little rolled oats and orris root powder. It helps to rub a little of the lavender oil on your hands when forming the soap mixture into a desired shape. Allow to dry on waxed paper in an airing cupboard.

Lavender and rose incense

1/4 teaspoon benzoin
1/4 teaspoon patchouli
1/4 teaspoon sandalwood
1 teaspoon cinnamon
1 teaspoon dried lavender flowers
1 teaspoon dried rose petals
1/2 cup water
1/4 teaspoon saltpetre

Grind the dry ingredients together in a mortar and pestle. Mix the water with the saltpetre and add 1½ teaspoons of this mixture to the previously ground ingredients. Mix together with a wooden ice cream stick. When the ingredients have formed a dough, the mixture may be formed into incense cones or it may be crumbled and sprinkled on the fire.

FLORAL FRAGRANCE

Tussie-mussies

These floral arrangements can carry messages in the language of flowers. In the past fragrant posies were often held to the nose to allay disease which was believed to have been carried by 'bad odours'. Tussie-mussies are exquisite tiny bouquets often made entirely with scented herbs.

Start with a central flower such as a rose bud or a scented pelargonium. Holding the central piece in one hand, surround it with lavender or foliage such as santolina, thrift or whatever takes the fancy and then twine either wool or cotton

Lavandula dentata and any of the Stoechas-type lavenders are often used for tussie-mussies but some of the dark-flowered *L. angustifolia* cultivars also create an attractive finish.

Lavender wreath

There are many ways of making wreaths. Here are two ideas to start with.

The first method uses very fine-meshed wire. Cut a strip of wire and mould it into a wreath shape, then fill with a fine dried moss (not sphagnum) or lichen. Push dried or fresh flowers and foliage with long stripped stems into the wreath and gradually build up the floral arrangement. This takes time but is well worth the effort. Dried flowers are often easier to use

Above and below: With these tussies mussies, a 'Cecile Brunner' *bloom has been progressively encircled by stems of L. stoechas and sage, and fringed by mint and pelargonium leaves*

around this central core to bind it together. Gradually build up the layers and finish with plant material which frames the tussie-mussie — scented pelargonium leaves, fennel leaves, grey-leaved senecio or statice create a stunning effect. Tie the wool or cotton at the base and trim the stems to the desired length. Frame the tussie-mussie with a lace doily and surround the cut stems with damp moss and enclose in foil.

Tussie-mussies are best made the day before they are to be used and left to stand overnight in water. A tussie-mussie will easily last a week and, depending on the material used, may be carefully dried to retain its colour. Alternatively, one can make a tussie-mussie from dried material although the fragrance will not be as potent.

CREATIVE IDEAS WITH LAVENDER

LAVENDER WREATH
The base of this wreath is dried L. angustifolia stems woven in a wire frame. Fresh L. stoechas stems have been added along with sprigs of fresh mint, thyme and three 'Cecile Brunner' blooms.

with this method as the stems are less difficult to press into the moss than fresh pliable ones.

A second method is to bind together twigs or branches into the shape of a wreath. Grape, wisteria and honeysuckle are suitable vines to use but they must be pliable. Soaking them first in warm water can make the job much easier. Plant material can then be hot-glued or tied on.

Ribbons, decorations and lace may be glued or pinned to the arrangement to create mood and focus attention on the occasion for which the wreath is intended.

ACCESSORISING WITH LAVENDER

Lavender can add much charm to a house and the number of uses to which it can be put are limited only by one's imagination.

Lavender plants, especially *L. dentata*, make attractive topiary specimens in pots on verandahs and steps, as the centre of a potted display or as a focal point in a room (preferably near an open sunny window).

Dried lavender flowers and stems can be arranged decoratively in old jars, teapots, hat boxes, bowls, cups, kettles, brandy glasses, coloured bottles, cane and willow baskets, brass containers, decorated trays and clay pots — the possibilities are endless.

Bowls of lavender and pot-pourri, lavender bags, lavender bottles, wreaths and displays of lavender artistry will combine to give an 'old world' charm to any house.

Lavender, linen and lace have been traditional accessories for many years and create a refreshing display whenever they are arranged together. Try tying long pieces of lace around bunches of dried lavender or arranging bowls of lavender pot-pourri, dried or fresh lavender arrangements or loose lavender heads on lace doilys. Use lavender as a central theme or decoration on a wooden table covered with a white linen tablecloth, or use lace, white tablecloths and lavender to draw attention to a fine old washstand or hall-stand. Place three sprigs of lavender with a linen napkin either inside a serviette ring or tied together with a ribbon to enhance a table setting.

Lavender candles

Melt two or three lavender-coloured candles in a saucepan. Alternatively, ordinary white candles can be melted with chopped purple-coloured crayons. Once melted, remove the candle wicks.

Add lavender oil and lavender flowers (dark-coloured ones are particularly suitable) to the melted wax. Combine thoroughly. Find a suitable mould, oil the sides and cut a hole in the base large enough for the wick to fit through. Tie the other end of the wick to a stick so that the wick remains straight and centred and carefully pour in the wax. Allow to set.

Alternatively, dip the wick into the pot of melted wax, allow this layer to set and continue the layering process until the candle is the desired shape. Pressed lavender flowers can be waxed on to the exterior of the completed candle.

APPENDIX

LAVENDER NURSERIES
The following are specialist suppliers of lavender plants.

AUSTRALIA
Nardoo Wholesale Nursery
(James and Anna Tyson)
45 Lahey Road Phone (07) 5545-2308
North Tambourine, Qld. 4272 Fax (07) 5545 2972

Bibbenluke Lodge Lavender
(John and Jan Illingworth)
Monaro Highway Phone (02) 6458-5235
Bibbenluke, N.S.W. 2632 Fax (02) 6458-5248

Cameron's Nursery (Andy and Sonja Cameron)
PO Box 124 Phone (02) 9655-1155
Galston, N.S.W. 2159 Fax (02) 9655-1024
(wholesale only)

Larkman Nurseries (Clive Larkman)
7 Jurat Road Phone (03) 9735-3831
Lilydale, Vic. 3140 Fax (03) 9739-6370

Lavandula Farmhouse (Carol White)
Hepburn/Newstead Road Ph/Fax (03) 5476-4393
Shepherd's Flat, Vic. 3461

Warratina Lavender Farm (Annemarie Manders)
Quayle Road Phone (03) 5964-4650
Wandin Yallock, Vic. 3139 Fax (03) 5964-4658

Yuulong Lavender Estate
(Edythe Anderson and Rosemary Holmes)
R.M.B.E. 1215 Phone (03) 5368-9453
Ballarat, Vic. 3352 Fax (03) 5368-9175

Bridewstowe Estate Lavender Farm
(Garry Cassidy)
296 Gillespies Road Phone (03) 6352-8182
Nabowla, Tas. 7254 Fax (03) 6352-8123

Cottage Herbs (Brian Noone)
Lyndon Road Phone/Fax (08) 284-7988
MacDonald Park, S.A. 5121

NEW ZEALAND
The Ploughman's Garden and Nursery
(Peter Carter)
Duff Road Phone (09) 235-9739
No. 2 RD, Waiuku Fax (09) 235-2659

The Lavender Patch (Annabel and Neil Allen)
301 Otara Road Phone/Fax (07) 315-7132
RD 1, Opotiki

Horrobin & Hodge (Wayne Horrobin)
RD 331 Phone (06) 362-6806
Manakau via Levin Fax (06) 362-6761

Smalehort Consultancy & Research
(Peter Smale)
PO Box 356 Phone/Fax (03) 528-9049
Motueka

Leighvander (Elsie Hall)
RD 1 Wairau Valley Phone (03) 572-2851
Blenheim Fax (03) 572-2841

Lavender Fields (Jim Curnow)
224 Beach Road Phone (03) 312-7220
Waikuku Beach, Canterbury

Lavenite Enterprises (Virginia McNaughton)
Lavender Downs
Lawford Road, West Melton Ph/Fax (03) 347-9520
RD6, Christchurch

Somerfields (Jenny Somervell)
PO Box 10-133 Mail order only:
Phillipstown, Christchurch $5.00 per catalogue
 or $8.00 annual subscription

Arbordale Nurseries
(Grace and Eoin Johnson)
Bush Road Phone (03) 489-7295
RD 2, Mosgiel Fax (03) 489-7219

Blue Mountain Nurseries (Hughes Family)
99 Bushy Hill Street Phone (03) 204-8250
Tapanui Fax (03) 204-8278

Marshwood Garden and Nursery
(Adair and Geoff Genge)
Leonard Road, West Plains Phone (03) 215-7672
No. 4 RD, Invercargill

79

INDEX

commercial growing 48, 50
container growing 55-8
culinary uses 71-3
cultivation 50, 51

fragrant uses 73-8

harvesting and drying 54, 55
hedges 58, 59

knot gardens 59-63

lavender accessories 78
lavender nurseries 79
Lavandula 'Avonview' 18, 24, 49
    L. 'Helmsdale' 19, 24, 49, 55, 61, 66
    L. 'Marshwood' 19, 24, 66
    L. 'Pippa' 18, 24
Lavandula x *allardii* 29, 44, 45, 46, 53, 66
Lavandula angustifolia 16, 25, 28, 29, 32, 33, 34, 35, 37, 40, 70, 77
    L. a. ssp. *angustifolia* 22, 25, 27, 28, 32, 36, 58, 63, 64
    L. a. ssp. *pyrenaica* 25, 27, 28
    L. a. 'Alba' 30, 36, 52, 58
    L. a. 'Avice Hill' 32, 34, 58, 63
    L. a. 'Blue Mountain' 35, 36, 56, 58, 63, 66
    L. a. 'Bosisto' 32, 35
    L. a. 'Bowles Early' 32, 33
    L. a. 'Folgate' 32, 34, 57
    L. a. 'Gray Lady' 31, 36, 52, 66
    L. a. 'Hidcote' 27, 34, 52, 64

L. a. 'Hidcote Blue' 34
L. a. 'Hidcote Pink' 34, 37
L. a. 'Irene Doyle' 33, 34, 58, 63
L. a. 'Lady' 33
L. a. 'Miss Donnington' 32, 33
L. a. 'Munstead' 32, 35, 53, 56, 57, 58, 60, 63, 70
L. a. 'Nana Alba' 30, 36, 56, 57, 63
L. a. 'Nana Atropurpurea' 31, 35, 37, 58, 64, 66
L. a. 'Rosea' 26, 36, 37, 52, 58, 64
L. a. 'Twickel Purple' 26, 33, 58
Lavandula canariensis 46, 47, 50
Lavandula dentata 9, 15, 16, 22, 23, 44, 45, 55, 59, 60, 63, 65, 76, 77, 78
    L. d. var. *candicans* 15, 22, 23, 55, 59, 60
Lavandula x *heterophylla* 29, 45, 46
Lavandula x *intermedia* 'Alba' 36, 44, 49
    L. x i. 'Arabian Night' 39, 41
    L. x i. 'Bogong' 38, 41
    L. x i. 'Chaix' 44
    L. x i. 'Dilly Dilly' 41, 43
    L. x i. 'Grappenhall' 41
    L. x i. 'Grey Hedge' 39, 44, 58, 59, 60
    L. x i. 'Grey Lady' 38, 40
    L. x i. 'Grosso' 40, 42, 50, 58, 59, 70
    L. x i. 'Impress Purple' 41, 56, 58
    L. x i. 'Old English' 39, 44

L. x i. 'Scottish Cottage' 39, 44, 58, 59
L. x i. 'Seal' 37, 38, 43, 49, 60
L. x i. 'Super' 40, 42, 64, 70
L. x i. 'Sussex' 38, 41
L. x i. 'Wilson's Giant' 41, 44
L. x i. 'Yuulung' 33, 38
Lavandula lanata 23, 29, 54, 57
Lavandula latifolia 10, 23, 25, 28, 29, 37, 45, 54
Lavandula multifida 45, 46, 47
Lavandula officinalis 25
Lavandula pedunculata 20, 21
Lavandula pinnata 47, 50
Lavandula spica 8, 10, 25, 28, 44
Lavandula stoechas 7, 8, 9, 10, 20, 24, 55, 71
    L. s. ssp. *caesia* 61
    L. s. ssp. *cariensis* 22
    L. s. ssp. *luisieri* 22
    L. s. ssp. *pedunculata* 20, 21
    L. s. ssp. *sampaiana* 22
    L. s. ssp. *stoechas* 14, 20, 21, 59
    L. s. ssp. *stoechas* 'Alba' 21, 57, 60
Lavandula vera 25
Lavandula viridis 14, 21, 22, 59, 70

medicinal uses 68-71

pests and diseases 51, 53
plant associations 63-7
propagation 54
pruning 53